At Issue

Should the Federal Government Bail Out Private Industry?

Other Books in the At Issue Series:

At Issue

Should the Federal Government Bail Out Private Industry?

David Haugen, Book Editor

GREENHAVEN PRESS
A part of Gale, Cengage Learning

GALE
CENGAGE Learning™

Detroit • New York • San Francisco • New Haven, Conn • Waterville, Maine • London

GALE
CENGAGE Learning™

Christine Nasso, *Publisher*
Elizabeth Des Chenes, *Managing Editor*

© 2010 Greenhaven Press, a part of Gale, Cengage Learning.

Gale and Greenhaven Press are registered trademarks used herein under license.

For more information, contact:
Greenhaven Press
27500 Drake Rd.
Farmington Hills, MI 48331-3535
Or you can visit our Internet site at gale.cengage.com

For product information and technology assistance, contact us at

Gale Customer Support, 1-800-877-4253
For permission to use material from this text or product, submit all requests online at
www.cengage.com/permissions

Further permissions questions can be emailed to permissionrequest@cengage.com

Articles in Greenhaven Press anthologies are often edited for length to meet page requirements. In addition, original titles of these works are changed to clearly present the main thesis and to explicitly indicate the author's opinion. Every effort is made to ensure that Greenhaven Press accurately reflects the original intent of the authors. Every effort has been made to trace the owners of copyrighted material.

Cover image © Images.com/Corbis.

LIBRARY OF CONGRESS CATALOGING-IN-PUBLICATION DATA

Should the federal government bail out private industry? / David Haugen, book editor.
    p. cm. -- (At issue)
    Includes bibliographical references and index.
    978-0-7377-4656-3 (hbk.)
    978-0-7377-4657-0 (pbk.)
    1. Industrial policy--United States--Juvenile literature. 2. Banks and banking--Government policy--United States--Juvenile literature. 3. Government lending--United States--Juvenile literature. 4. Economic stabilization--United States--Juvenile literature. 5. United States--Economic policy--2009--Juvenile literature.
    I. Haugen, David M., 1969-
      HD3616.U47S46 2010
      338.5'430973--dc22

                                                    2009037781

Printed in the United States of America
1 2 3 4 5 6 7 13 12 11 10 09

Contents

Introduction

The ongoing global financial crisis that caused investment markets to plummet in 2008 began in 2006 when the housing boom in America came to an end. Property values had climbed steadily from around 1994, and more and more Americans took out mortgages to buy first homes—and even second homes, as well as investment properties. Over this same period, consumer debt was growing as lending companies expanded credit to millions of Americans who charged at unprecedented levels. By 2005, the majority of Americans were using nearly all of their disposable income to buy consumer goods or pay interest on loans. Little of their money was going towards savings plans. But even these cash-strapped citizens could acquire mortgages thanks to banks' and mortgage companies' easy credit terms. Lenders tempted prospective homebuyers with no-money-down mortgages at low adjustable rates (instead of 30-year fixed rates), and they extended such loans to "subprime" borrowers—homebuyers who had poor credit and low-paying or unstable job histories.

About half of these subprime mortgages were bought up by the Federal National Mortgage Association (Fannie Mae) and the Federal Home Loan Mortgage Corporation (Freddie Mac), two government-sponsored enterprises that sold shares to stockholders. The other half of these subprime mortgages were bundled together with stable mortgages and sold as mortgage-backed securities on Wall Street. Many investment companies and foreign investors snapped up these securities because the return on them had traditionally been strong during the housing boom. The strong demand for these securities—from the government enterprises and private investment houses—influenced lenders to continue to offer mortgages to nearly anyone who asked for one. But when the terms of the adjustable rate mortgages changed (usually after three to five years), many subprime borrowers could not afford the new higher rates. Household incomes were not rising to meet the inordinate amount of consumer debt. Troubled homeowners went into bankruptcy, and more than 2 million properties went into foreclosure. Banks and mortgage companies lost income, and thus the value of mortgage-backed securities plummeted. Suffering estimated losses that range from $285 billion (Standard & Poor's) to $600 billion (UBS), banks and financial giants began restricting consumer credit, making it even more difficult for cash-poor Americans to pay bills and invest in the economy. At the same time, global investors were stung with hundreds of billions of dollars in losses, leading to a worldwide panic and credit freeze.

As credit lines shrank and investment houses collapsed, American unemployment rose from just over 5 percent in 2008 to 8.1 percent in 2009—a fifteen-year high, according to the Bureau of Labor Statistics. Consumer spending declined by more than 3 percent, and the U.S. economy slowed significantly in the 2008–2009 transition. At the same time the economy was shifting, the presidential administration was undergoing change. On his way out of office, George W. Bush bore the brunt of the market collapse. In a weekly radio address in November 2008, Bush spread the blame for the crisis around to speculators, government, and the American people. He stated, "It is true that this crisis included failures by lenders and borrowers, by financial firms, by governments and independent regulators. But the crisis was not a failure of the free market system." Bush asserted that free market capitalism would eventually right itself with careful scrutiny and appropriate regulation. Until such a time, he proposed and signed a $700 billion bailout package to help keep banks and investment firms afloat by authorizing the Treasury to buy up bad mortgage securities. Still, he warned, "We must recognize that government intervention is not a cure-all" and that "the long-term solution to today's problems is sustained economic growth."

Critics of the Bush recovery plan argued that $700 billion was simply being handed over to risky speculators who failed to invest wisely. Even worse, the package was being delivered with few strings attached, and there was little oversight of how the government money (that is, taxpayer money) was to be spent. While most Americans waited for a loosening of credit, some Wall Street firms that received tens of billions in bailout money seemed more interested in financing deals overseas in China, India, and the Middle East. Representative Dennis J. Kucinich from Ohio maintained, "When the American people find that their tax dollars, which were supposed to be used to get us out of this financial crisis, instead are being used to ship jobs and investments overseas, there will be outrage."

Incoming President Barack Obama was also critical of how the bailout money was being used, and he feared that the country would see this necessary measure as a waste of taxpayer goodwill. He vowed that the second half of the $700 billion (which was released to the government in January 2009) would come with more oversight to ensure that the money was put in the service of homeowners and small businesses. "We can regain the confidence of both Congress and the American people in that this is not just money that is being given to banks without any strings attached and nobody knows what happens," Obama said, "but rather that it is targeted very specifically at getting credit flowing again to businesses and families." But Obama's rhetoric has also drawn fire, especially regarding his administration's pledge to stem the tide of foreclosures. Many homeowners who bought homes within their budgets and took out fixed interest loans are angered that their tax money is being used to help keep subprime borrowers in homes they obviously could not afford. One Seattle homebuyer told the Associated Press, "I feel like I'm doing the right thing paying my mortgage, and now apparently I have to pay my neighbor's mortgage, too." Indeed, Obama's plan is to use $75 billion in incentives for banks to refinance subprime mortgages so that 4 million Americans will not face foreclosure in the near future. The administration also hopes the move will halt falling home values so that homeowners will not continue to witness ever-shrinking property values.

In addition to helping banks and homeowners, the Obama administration is also being hounded by U.S. automakers for part of the bailout package. In December 2008, President Bush signed over $17.4 billion in loans to General Motors (GM) and Chrysler, which along with Ford make up the Big Three of American car manufacturers. Both companies claimed that poor sales were bringing them near to bankruptcy and that a rescue package was needed to avoid the demise of an American institution as well as the widespread unemployment it would entail. Stating that this decline "would worsen a weak job market and exacerbate the financial crisis," Bush agreed to the loans on the condition that GM and Chrysler restructure and prove to the government that they could remain profitable. In February 2009, the automakers petitioned President Obama for $21.6 billion more in aid, claiming that bankruptcy was imminent. The new administration made no immediate decision, while lawmakers were divided on the issue. Some believed the industry could not be allowed to fall, while others were not convinced that GM and Chrysler had yet to make good on their promises to cut costs and work out pay and benefit issues with their unions. However, Obama did release $5 billion in assistance to car part suppliers, hinting strongly that the administration sees U.S. automakers as a necessary part of a healthy economy. While negotiations went on, Chrysler filed for bankruptcy protection in April 2009 and merged with the European carmaker Fiat. General Motors meanwhile sold many of its assets as it plunged into bankruptcy, emerging in July 2009 as a reformed company, still holding its debts to the federal government.

Despite the fact that these bailouts are moving through Congress and gaining the approval of the sitting president, the public is still not united behind the notion that banks, auto makers, and even private homeowners have the right to expect government assistance when their business ventures or high risk gambles do not pay off. After all, most businesses in the United States are allowed to fail if they cannot remain profitable, and average homeowners are expected to purchase property within their means or forfeit their investment to the lender who put up the money. As Steve Berg, a former Washington, D.C., bureau writer for the Minneapolis-St. Paul *Star Tribune*, writes, "The problem with all of this intervention— whether it's government help for lenders, builders or at-risk homeowners—is that it seems to reward the very behavior that caused the problem." In *At Issue: Should the Federal Government Bail Out Private Industry?* various commentators examine the issue, and many side with Berg's view that bailouts prove that there are no consequences for irresponsible investments. However, some observers contend that allowing Wall Street, major industry, and millions of homeowners to go under would do far too much harm to the country. "The problem is that, as a country, we can't make decisions based simply on anger or capitalistic dogma," states Richard Gibbons, one of the authors quoted in this book. "We have a responsibility to do whatever will help ensure this country's future prosperity." Gibbons's opinion seems to match that of President Obama, who said in February 2008, "All of us will pay an even steeper price if we allow this crisis to deepen—a crisis which is unraveling homeownership, the middle class, and the American Dream itself. But if we act boldly and swiftly to arrest this downward spiral, every American will benefit." Indeed, all Americans are hoping that the taxpayer-funded bailout— whether just or unjust—will do something to avert a deepening crisis and restore jobs, home values, and faith in the American Dream.

1

The Government Bank Bailout Plan Is Necessary

Richard Gibbons

Richard Gibbons is an investor and a contributor to The Motley Fool, an online and print investment advice news service.

While the U.S. government's 2008 bailout of failing banks flies in the face of the nation's capitalist principles, it is a necessary evil. Without shoring up these financial institutions with taxpayer dollars, the country would have witnessed an economic collapse that would have left taxpayers cleaning up the mess anyway. In addition, a banking collapse would have restricted the flow of credit, forcing businesses to go under and bringing about greater unemployment. The government's aid will likely restore consumer confidence in the banking system and lead to a return of lending and general recovery.

A lot of people have been complaining about the bailouts. This is understandable. The basis of capitalism is that the strong survive, while the weak collapse. It's galling to see people rewarded for failure.

The problem is that, as a country, we can't make decisions based simply on anger or capitalistic dogma. We have a responsibility to do whatever will help ensure this country's future prosperity. And right now, that means bailing out the banks, increasing regulation, and stimulating the economy.

Capitalism's Blind Spot

Capitalism works well, generally allocating resources efficiently. It's the reason why there's usually food on the supermarket shelves, while there often wasn't in the U.S.S.R. [Soviet Union].

But capitalism has its blind spots, too. In a capitalist system, it's rational for bank executives to take huge risks in order to pad bonuses based on short-term metrics. Bank executives don't care about systemic risks—often they barely care about their own shareholders. So, regulation is necessary to reduce systemic risk.

Unfortunately, our regulators disliked regulation, and [in 2008], the resulting crisis drove the banking system to the brink of collapse.

Without government assistance, it seems likely that most of the top-tier banks would have collapsed.

House of Cards

And I really mean collapse. Of the big five investment banks, only Morgan Stanley and Goldman Sachs are still standing, with Lehman, Bear Stearns, and Merrill Lynch all either bankrupt or sold.

Same with the biggest retail banks. Citigroup fell from over $50 per share to under $5 per share despite huge cash infusions, and Bank of America looks to be getting there. Wachovia, the fourth-biggest bank, was acquired. Washington Mutual [WaMu], the sixth-biggest, became the biggest failure in U.S. banking history.

Without government assistance, it seems likely that most of the top-tier banks would have collapsed. As if that weren't enough, the Bank Insurance Fund (BIF)—which provides deposit insurance—has less than $100 billion, enough to cover only 1.01% of outstanding deposits. Citigroup alone has over

$600 billion in deposits. By itself, Washington Mutual would have drained the BIF if the Federal Deposit Insurance Corp. hadn't used sleight of hand to transfer WaMu's operations to JPMorgan.

With widespread bank failures, deposit insurance would falter, and the taxpayers would be footing the bill regardless. That's why we see all these acquisitions—because the banking system can't handle the failures. It's cheaper for the country to just save the banks.

If we do let the banks go under, there will be huge problems, because our whole economic system runs on credit.

The Domino Effect

If we do let the banks go under, there will be huge problems, because our whole economic system runs on credit. How many small companies use lines of credit to handle seasonality in their businesses? How many large companies rely on sales of commercial paper? If that money is unavailable, many completely viable businesses will go under because of liquidity issues.

Any company that uses debt is vulnerable. Procter & Gamble is practically invincible in any normal situation. But it has $35 billion in net debt. What happens when its lenders ask for some of that money back, and it has to borrow at 15% to get the cash? Wal-Mart has $41 billion in net debt. When nobody wants to lend, how do you borrow $41 billion?

What happens when the farmers, truckers, and other businesses making up the backbone of our infrastructure, fail? Will there still be food on the supermarket shelves? I don't know, but I'm not eager to find out.

A New Deal

In fact, the history of the Great Depression shows what happens when you start killing the banking system. Between 1929 and 1933, about one in five banks went under. As you'd expect, these bank failures took a massive toll on the economy, with real GDP [gross domestic product] falling by 29% and unemployment hitting 25%.

At that point, President Franklin Roosevelt stepped in with a plan called the "New Deal." He shut down the banks and allowed only sound banks to reopen. He passed the Emergency Banking Act, which made federal loans available to banks. Then, he enacted the Glass-Steagall Act, establishing deposit insurance and preventing depository banks from being investment banks, reducing the risk of banks blowing up because of bad investments. (Unfortunately, Glass-Steagall was repealed in 1999, which is one reason why banks were able to trade asset-backed securities (ABS) and blow up the system nine years later.)

After these actions restored confidence in the banking system, Roosevelt focused on employment through numerous public works projects and agricultural programs.

The results of this government intervention were impressive. GDP skyrocketed from 1933 to 1937, posting real growth of 9.4% annually—a huge rate for a developed country. Unemployment fell to 14.3%.

Reasons for Optimism

[Billionaire investor] Warren Buffett knows this history, and that's probably why he said that the bank bailout was "absolutely necessary to avoid going over the precipice." Now he's confident that America will bounce back.

The government's actions have helped to restore confidence in the banking system—a TED spread [a credit risk indicator] down from 5 to 1 indicates that banks are more willing to lend to each other now than any time since September [2008]. Now, President [Barack] Obama, like Roosevelt, is working on programs to help Americans get back to work.

To me, it seems likely that these government interventions will pave the road to recovery. The world's richest man [Buffett] seems to agree, and says that if stocks continue to trade at bargain prices, he'll put his entire personal portfolio into equities. That's why I think now is the time to find undervalued stocks, invest, and grow rich.

2

The Government Bank Bailout Plan Is a Fraud

Chuck Baldwin

Chuck Baldwin is a pastor who has turned to radio broadcasts and syndicated columns to comment on politics and current events from his conservative Christian point of view. He ran in the 2008 presidential election as a member of the Constitution Party, a political ticket that supports the ideals of America's Founding Fathers.

The government's 2008 banking bailout is a fraud perpetrated on the American people. The government has abandoned sound money practices in favor of allowing the Federal Reserve—a banking cartel—to dictate fiscal policy. These unscrupulous bankers take advantage of profits when the economy is good and pass the burden onto the taxpayers when the economy turns bad. The government should do away with the Federal Reserve and return the nation to a banking system based on hard assets if America is to survive the current financial crisis.

At the time of this writing [in September 2008], the U.S. House and Senate are poised to pass a $700 billion bailout to Wall Street. At the behest of President George W. Bush, the U.S. taxpayers are going to be on the hook for what can only be referred to as the biggest fraud in U.S. history.

Virtually our entire financial system is based on an illusion. We spend more than we earn, we consume more than we produce, we borrow more than we save, and we cling to the fantasy that this can go on forever. The glue that holds this crumbling scheme together is a fiat currency known as the Federal Reserve Note, which was created out of thin air by an international banking cartel called the Federal Reserve.

According to Congressman Ron Paul [of Texas], in the last three years, the Federal Reserve [the Fed] has created over $4 trillion in new money. The result of all this "money-out-of-thin-air" fraud is never-ending inflation. And the more prices rise, the more the dollar collapses. Folks, this is not sustainable.

The Evils of the Banking Cartel

Already, Bear Stearns was awarded a $29 billion bailout, followed quickly by the bailout of Freddie and Fannie[1] that will cost the taxpayers up to $200 billion. Then the Fed announced the bailout of AIG [American International Group, Inc.] to the tune of $85 billion. Mind you, AIG is an enormous global entity with assets totaling more than $1.1 trillion. Moreover, the Feds agreed to pump $180 billion into global money markets. And the Treasury Department promised $50 billion to insure the holdings of money market mutual funds for a year. Now, taxpayers are being asked to provide $700 billion to Wall Street. (I hope readers are aware that, not only will American banks be bailed out, but foreign banks will also be bailed out. Then again, at least half of the Federal Reserve is comprised of foreign banks, anyway.) In other words, the Federal Reserve is preparing to spend upwards of $1 trillion or more. Remember again, this is fiat money, meaning it is money printed out of thin air.

All of this began when the U.S. Congress abrogated its responsibility to maintain sound money principles on behalf of

---

1. Freddie Mac is the nickname for Federal Home Loan Mortgage Corporation; Fannie Mae is the nickname for Federal National Mortgage Association; both companies buy mortgages from banks and other lenders.

the American people (as required by the Constitution) and created the Federal Reserve. This took place in 1913. The President was Woodrow Wilson. (I strongly encourage readers to buy G. Edward Griffin's book, *The Creature from Jekyll Island.*) Since then, the U.S. economy has suffered through one Great Depression and several recessions—all of which have been orchestrated by this international banking cartel. Now, we are facing total economic collapse.

No matter how bad it gets on Main Street, the banksters on Wall Street will still have the best of it.

But don't worry: the international bankers will lose nothing—not even their bonuses. They will maintain their mansions, yachts, private jets, and Swiss bank accounts. No matter how bad it gets on Main Street, the banksters on Wall Street will still have the best of it—President Bush and the Congress will make sure of that. This is one thing Republicans and Democrats can agree on.

The Founding Fathers Sounded the Warning

America's founders were rightfully skeptical of granting too much power to bankers. Thomas Jefferson said, "If the American people ever allow private banks to control the issuance of their currency, first by inflation and then by deflation, the banks and corporations that will grow up around them will deprive the people of all their property until their children will wake up homeless on the continent their fathers conquered."

Jefferson also believed that "banking establishments are more dangerous than standing armies; and that the principle of spending money to be paid by posterity, under the name of funding, is but swindling futurity on a large scale."

Daniel Webster [one of America's Founding Fathers] warned, "Of all the contrivances for cheating the laboring classes of mankind, none has been more effectual than that which deludes them with paper money."

Webster also said, "We are in danger of being overwhelmed with irredeemable paper, mere paper, representing not gold nor silver; no, Sir, representing nothing but broken promises, bad faith, bankrupt corporations, cheated creditors, and a ruined people."

Our first and greatest President George Washington said, "Paper money has had the effect in your State [Rhode Island] that it ever will have, to ruin commerce—oppress the honest, and open the door to every species of fraud and injustice."

The only way to fix this economic mess that the international bankers have created is to return America to sound money principles.

Send the Bankers to Jail

If George W. Bush, [2008 presidential candidate] John McCain, or [2008 presidential candidate] Barack Obama had any honesty and integrity, they would approach the current banking malady in much the same way that President Andrew Jackson did. In discussing the Bank Renewal bill with a delegation of bankers in 1832, Jackson said, "Gentlemen, I have had men watching you for a long time, and I am convinced that you have used the funds of the bank to speculate in the breadstuffs of the country. When you won, you divided the profits amongst you, and when you lost, you charged it to the bank. You tell me that if I take the deposits from the bank and annul its charter, I shall ruin ten thousand families. That may be true, gentlemen, but that is your sin! Should I let you go on, you will ruin fifty thousand families, and that would be my sin! You are a den of vipers and thieves. I intend to rout you out, and by the eternal God, I will rout you out."

What President Andrew Jackson said to the bankers in 1832 is exactly what an American President should say to these criminal international bankers today. But what George Bush, John McCain, and Barack Obama want to do is provide amnesty for the international bankers, just as they want to provide amnesty for illegal aliens. I say, no amnesty for Wall Street, and no amnesty for illegal aliens, either. Instead of sending these banksters on extended vacations to the Bahamas with millions of taxpayer dollars in their pockets, we should be sending them straight to jail!

The only way to fix this economic mess that the international bankers have created is to return America to sound money principles, as prescribed in the U.S. Constitution. This means dismantling the Federal Reserve and the Internal Revenue Service, overturning the 16th Amendment and the personal income tax, and returning the American monetary system to hard assets: gold and silver. Anything short of this will only delay and worsen the inevitable collapse that has already begun.

3

The Government Bank Bailout Plan Subsidizes Swindlers

James Petras

James Petras is an emeritus professor of sociology at Binghamton University in New York. He is a widely published author with numerous articles and 63 book credits to his name. His latest book, Rulers and Ruled in the U.S. Empire, *was published in 2007.*

The government was wrong to authorize a bailout of U.S. banking institutions. By making these banks' debts a public burden, the government has allowed the swindlers to escape punishment and forced the taxpayer to subsidize bankers' wrongdoings. Such a plan will embolden the swindlers to continue to cheat the system, knowing that their actions have no personal repercussions. The government should have used the bailout money to invest in health care, industry, education, or other elements of the national infrastructure that will generate tangible benefits for the economy.

Treasury Secretary [Henry] Paulson and President [George W.] Bush backed by the Democratic Congressional leadership have asked Congress for $700 billion dollars to bail out Wall Street financial institutions.

Over the past several years these banks reaped billions of dollars borrowing and speculating on mortgages, securities and other financial paper with virtually no capital covering their bets. With the fall in the housing market, Wall Street's financial debts skyrocketed, the value of their holdings evaporated and they are saddled with trillions of dollars of debt.

Paulson, Bush and the Congressional leadership want the US taxpayer to buy Wall Street's worthless private debts, saddling current and future generations of US taxpayers with worthless paper.

Paulson/Bush and the Congressional leaders falsely claim that failure to bail out the Wall Street swindlers will lead to the collapse of the financial system. In fact, almost 200 of our leading economists from the most prestigious universities reject Paulson's bailout. The truth of the matter is that withholding funds to Wall Street will lead to the collapse of the swindler-speculator-run financial system, which created the current economic debacle.

Bailing out swindlers only encourages more swindling.

Opportunity for Public Oversight

The Federal Government can and should use the hundreds of billions of public money to establish a national, publicly controlled banking and investment system subject to oversight by elected representatives. The collapse of the current bankrupt financial system is both a threat and an opportunity: The collapse of this corrupt system has led to the loss of jobs and frozen credit and lending; the establishment of a new publicly owned banking system offers an opportunity to finance the priorities of the vast majority of the American people: the re-industrialization of our economy, a universal national health program, securing and extending social security into the next century, rebuilding our decaying infrastructure and many other programs essential to the American way of life.

The problem is not the false alternative of bailing out Wall Street or financial chaos and collapse: The real choice is between subsidizing swindlers or establishing a responsible, responsive and equitable publicly run financial system.

The channeling of funds to Wall Street will divert funds from getting us out of this deepening recession.

Ten Reasons to Oppose the Wall Street Bailout

1. In a market economy capitalists justify their profits by the risk of losses that they take. Gamblers cannot keep their profits and pass their losses to the taxpayers. They have to take responsibility for their bad decisions.

2. Much of the toxic (garbage) debts were based on fraudulent practices—opaque financial instruments unrelated to real assets (but which generated huge commissions). Bailing out swindlers only encourages more swindling.

3. The US Treasury will purchase worthless paper, the private banks will retain any assets of value. We buy the lemons, they drive the Cadillacs.

4. The chance of the Treasury recovering any value from their purchases of bad debt is near zero. The taxpayers will be stuck with paper with no buyers.

5. The long-term effect of a bailout will be to double the public debt and undercut funding for Social Security, Medicare, Medicaid, education and public health programs while increasing the tax burden of future generations.

6. The dollar will devalue as the government debt will decrease its attractiveness overseas, increasing the cost of imports and resulting in an inflationary spiral which will further undermine working people's living standards.

7. The channeling of funds to Wall Street will divert funds from getting us out of this deepening recession.

8. The bailout will deepen the financial crisis because, according to the Director of the Congressional Budget Office, it will expose the fact that many institutions may be carrying many more 'toxic assets' and reveal that those institutions are not solvent. In other words, the Treasury and Congress are freeing up bad debts to insolvent institutions.

9. The bailout is aimed at facilitating lending; but if the problem is not credit but (as the Congressional Budget Office has shown) the insolvency of the financial institutions, the solution is to create solvent financial institutions.

10. The bailout totally ignores the financial needs of 10 million homeowners facing foreclosures, the bankruptcy of small enterprises facing a credit crunch and the loss of workers' jobs and health plans for their families because of the recession.

Alternatives to the Wall Street Bailout

The speed with which this gigantic amount of public funds had been made available by the Treasury and Congress puts the lie to their argument that popular programs cannot be funded or need to be cut back. In fact, investing $700 billion in the health and education of American workers will increase productivity, open markets and expand consumer power leading to a virtuous circle increasing public revenues and eliminating the budget and trade deficits.

Public funds invested in manufacturing, construction, education and health care leads to products with real use value and has a multiplier effect on the rest of the economy instead of ending up in the pockets of billionaires who speculate and invest in mergers and overseas buyouts.

The Treasury and Congress have inadvertently revealed that federal financing is readily available to rebuild the US economy, guarantee decent living wages and provide health care for everyone *if* we choose elective officials who are committed to the needs of the US workers and not the Wall Street billionaires.

4

Bailout Money Should Not Be Used to Pay Executive Bonuses

Nomi Prins

Nomi Prins is a journalist and senior fellow at Demos, a public policy center. Her articles have appeared in the New York Times, Newsday, *and* The Nation. *She is also the author of* Other People's Money *and* Jacked: How "Conservatives" are Picking Your Pocket (Whether You Voted for Them or Not).

Many banking institutions that are slated to receive money from the government bailout plan expect to utilize part of the funds to pay executive bonuses. This is particularly offensive given that small businesses and average citizens are suffering under the economic downturn while Wall Street CEOs seem to be immune to its effects. The White House needs to make good on its promise to make sure bankers are not profiting from the crisis that is crippling millions of taxpayers.

The [2008] election results pretty much confirmed the extent to which Main Street is rightly livid about the Wall Street mentality that led to our financial crisis. During his historic victory speech, President-elect Barack Obama told supporters, and the rest of the world, "If this financial crisis taught us anything, it's that we cannot have a thriving Wall Street while Main Street suffers."

But, it seems that Wall Street didn't get that memo. It turns out that the nine banks about to be getting a total equity capital injection of $125 billion, courtesy of Phase I of The Bailout Plan, had reserved $108 billion during the first nine months of 2008 in order to pay for compensation and bonuses.

Not Part of the Plan

Paying Wall Street bonuses was not supposed to be part of the plan. At least that's how Federal Reserve Chairman Ben Bernanke and Treasury Secretary Hank Paulson explained it to Congress and the American people. So, on Oct. 1, when the Senate, including Obama, approved the $700 billion bailout package, the illusion was that this would magically loosen the credit markets, and with taxpayer-funded relief, banks would first start lending to each other again, and then, to citizens and small businesses. And all would be well.

Whereas Wall Street may not believe in higher taxes for the richest citizens, it does believe in higher bonuses for the head honchos.

That didn't happen. Which is why it's particularly offensive that the no-strings-attached money is going to line the pockets of Wall Street execs. The country's top investment bank (which since Sept. 21 calls itself a bank holding company), Goldman Sachs, set aside $11.4 billion during the first nine months of this year [2008]—slightly more than the firm's $10 billion U.S. government gift—to cover bonus payments for its 443 senior partners, who are set to make about $5 million each, and other employees.

Whereas Wall Street may not believe in higher taxes for the richest citizens, it does believe in higher bonuses for the head honchos. No matter what the market conditions are on the outside, steadfast feelings of entitlement tend to prevail.

Last year [in 2007], when the financial crisis was just brewing, the top five investment banks paid themselves $39 billion in compensation and bonuses, up 6 percent over 2006. Goldman's CEO, Lloyd C. Blankfein, bagged a record bonus of $60.7 million, including $26.8 million in cash. That amount was nearly double the $38 million that Paulson made at the firm in 2005, the year before he became the Treasury secretary, a post for which he received unanimous approval from the Senate on June 28, 2006.

Two of those firms, Bear Stearns and Lehman Brothers, went bankrupt this year. Bank of America is acquiring a third, Merrill Lynch. Shares in the remaining two, Morgan Stanley and Goldman Sachs, took a 60 percent nosedive this year.

Yet, that didn't stop their campaign contribution money from spewing out. Goldman was Obama's largest corporate campaign contributor, with $874,207. Also in his top 20 were three other recipients of bailout capital: JP Morgan/Chase, Citigroup and Morgan Stanley.

[Banks] have been subtly releasing data to the media regarding how much lower bonuses will be this year, in order to combat inspection and criticism.

Investigations into Bonus Plays

Last week [in late October 2008], House Oversight Committee Chairman Henry Waxman, D-Calif., gave the bailout capital recipient firms until Nov. 10 to come up with some darn good reasons to be paying themselves so much. Specifically, he requested detailed information on the total and average compensation per year from 2006 to 2008, the number of employees expected to be paid more than $500,000 in total compensation, and the total compensation projected for the top 10 executives.

Similarly, New York state Attorney General Andrew Cuomo demanded information about this year's bonuses, including a detailed accounting of expected payments to top management and the size of the firms' expected bonus pool before and after knowing that they would be recipients of taxpayer funds.

The deadline Cuomo set for receiving bonus records was Nov. 5. Predictably, the firms in question requested more time as the date approached—it takes a while to massage numbers, after all.

Meanwhile, they have been subtly releasing data to the media regarding how much lower bonuses will be this year, in order to combat inspection and criticism. This is Wall Street in its best defense mode, projecting an aura of accommodation and self-pity (because it's shedding jobs, too), in order to maintain a status quo state of self-regulation.

House Financial Service Committee Chairman Barney Frank is holding his own oversight hearing on the matter next week, having announced that "any use of these funds for any purpose other than lending—for bonuses, for severance pay, for dividends, for acquisitions of other institutions, etc.—is a violation of the terms" of the bailout plan.

How Banks Are Likely to Avoid Blame

Banks are going to tell Congress that of course they won't use that $125 billion for bonuses—it will go to shoring up balance sheets and for acquisitions just like they promised. And bonus money will come from earnings, as it always does.

If it sounds like accounting mumbo-jumbo, that's because it is. It doesn't matter where in the balance sheet capital comes from or goes, the point is there's more of it because of taxpayer redistribution in the wrong direction than there would have been otherwise, and that's not just. This begs the larger question: Why pay bonuses in a year of massive financial destruction, anyway?

"Exactly," says Gar Alperovitz, co-author, with Lew Daly, of the new book *Unjust Deserts*. "We're making homeowners take a big hit, and if there's any justification for any of these bonuses—which is dubious—sharing that burden is important."

But that's not quite the sharing that Wall Street wanted from the bailout package. Yet, if "change has come to America," as per Obama's promise, then it's high time for Wall Street to shoulder its part—starting with this bonus season. A decisive move by Obama on this topic would go a long way toward solidifying the central promise of his campaign.

5

Bailed-out Banks Should Pay Promised Bonuses to Their Executives

Terence Corcoran

Terence Corcoran is the editor and columnist for the Financial Post, *a section of Toronto's* National Post *newspaper. He is the coauthor of* Public Money, Private Greed, *a book he wrote with Laura Reid.*

It is wrong to blame bankers and other corporate heads for the economic meltdown that followed a market-wide failure in 2008. As government financial analysts have stated, the collapse cannot be traced solely to banking and investment speculations; the entire market regulation system shares the blame as well as the monitors who failed to take heed of warning signs. Banking institutions, therefore, should not be persecuted for honoring employee contracts that require them to pay out yearly bonuses for good work. These bonuses help banks keep their talent pools and also help draw in new talent. It is poor policy to believe that restricting such bonus payments will somehow redress the failures of the whole global market.

To use a current cliché, frequently deployed to humiliate bankers and CEOs: He doesn't get it. Barack Obama, that is. He just doesn't get it, and nor do millions of others who are following the U.S. President on his long destructive march against bankers and corporate executives for their alleged "recklessness and greed."

Those were the words Mr. Obama used yesterday [March 15, 2009] when he instructed his treasury secretary, Timothy Geithner, to "pursue every legal avenue" to block the payment of $165 million in bonuses to employees of AIG Financial Products. News of the payments sparked a demagogic explosion in Congress and the U.S. media, and the President seized the momentum and then got out in front of it. He loves a parade.

Companies Should Compensate the Best Employees

There's no need to repeat here the distorted content and hysterical tone of the AIG [American International Group, Inc.] explosion. What is worth repeating, however, are some of the facts behind the AIG bonus payments. Much has been made of AIG CEO Edward Liddy's letter to Mr. Geithner, explaining the reasons for the bonuses. For people who like facts with their hysteria, and can calm down enough to read it, the Liddy letter appears [in the March 16, 2009 *Financial Post*].

The attack on executive compensation, Wall Street bonuses and bankers is largely without merit.

Mr. Liddy had no involvement with establishing the original bonus plan, designed to "retain" AIG Financial Product specialists through 2008 and 2009. But he says he has "grave concerns about the long-term consequences of the actions we are taking" to reduce the contractual payments to AIG employees. He warns of AIG's inability to retain the best talent. AIG, he says, will simply not be able to attract employees if they come to believe "that their compensation is subject to continued and arbitrary adjustment by the U.S. Treasury."

Now their compensation is about to undergo adjustment down to zero by the U.S. President. They say you can't fight city hall. Then what can you do with the mighty U.S. government, which is going to throw the full legal force of the state against you? Even if the AIG employees are legally and rightly entitled to their bonus payments—which they almost certainly are—they are about to get steamrolled by a populist president riding an anti-corporate wave.

A Misguided Attack on the Private Sector

Of course, if you believe that AIG and its Financial Products group—through greed, recklessness and malfeasance—were the cause of AIG's failure and the adjacent global financial meltdown, then you have no problem with rolling back the bonuses.

But the attack on executive compensation, Wall Street bonuses and bankers is largely without merit, a trumped up attack on the private sector—on markets and capitalism—to overshadow the real causes of the global financial crisis. In recent weeks, reports from U.S. Fed [Federal Reserve System] Chairman Ben Bernanke, the International Monetary Fund [IMF] and former Fed Chairman Alan Greenspan added to the already mountainous body of evidence that massive government failure created a monetary- and policy-driven house of cards.

Writing in *The Wall Street Journal* last week [March 2009], Mr. Greenspan all but conceded that the Fed missed the signals and implications from the flood of foreign-owned dollars cascading into the U.S. market—dollars that his monetary policies had created. But he said his 1% interest rate regime through 2003 and 2004 was not to blame.

Then Mr. Bernanke, current Fed chairman, in a speech last Tuesday [March 10, 2009], said we were experiencing the worst financial crisis since the 1930s, but, "Its fundamental causes remain in dispute." While corporate behaviour may have played a role, Mr. Bernanke ran through a list of government-based causes for the global crisis. Mr. Bernanke cited global savings imbalances, the buildup of U.S. dollar currency reserves in China and elsewhere and the buildup of oil dollars among petroleum exporting countries.

The buildup of systemic risk—the rising odds that the entire system might crash—took place beyond the ability or even the responsibility of any one private bank or insurance company. No bankers or AIG executives are responsible for systemic risk.

The private sector, bankers and insurance companies were the victims of a failed global financial regulatory regime.

Bankers Are Victims of the Economic Crisis

The leading government-created disaster behind the financial crisis is U.S. housing policy and the multi-trillion dollar securitized mortgage market created by the U.S.-government backed mortgage agencies known as Fannie Mae [Federal National Mortgage Association] and Freddie Mac [Federal Home Loan Mortgage Corporation]. In comments in 2007, Mr. Bernanke reported that the two agencies, with $5.2-trillion in mortgage obligations, posed a systemic risk. Such risk, he said, occurs when "disruptions occurring in one firm or financial market may spread to other parts of the financial system, with possibly serious implications for the performance of the broader economy."

When Fannie Mae and Freddie Mac failed because of the mortgage bubble they helped create, the systemic meltdown spread around the globe. The private sector, bankers and insurance companies were the victims of a failed global financial regulatory regime.

That conclusion is essentially the one delivered by International Monetary Fund officials in early March. In a brief report, "Initial Lessons of the Crisis," the IMF reviews the regulatory disaster. It tries to put the blame on "market failure" and financial institutions for failing to recognize the looming systemic problems. But it is the regulators—who are really charged with detecting and preventing systemic risks—who failed to see the train coming down the track.

Botched regulations, distorting accounting rules, misguided monetary policy, over-stimulative government policy—the list of state policy failure behind the crisis is long and much more significant than any of the individual deals done by AIG Financial Products. They sold products that made sense under the monetary and regulatory regimes established by governments all over the world. Market players do that. Bankers are not responsible for systemic risk.

Undeserved Punishment

But now, apparently, bankers and financial market actors are supposed to personally pay for the government-created systemic risk and collapse. In its report, the IMF suggested that in future, financial market compensation packages should be designed so that individuals are only paid the money after the passage of time. "An early priority should be to delink bonuses from annual results and short-term indicators." Instead, bonuses would be paid as "deferred disbursements and allowing for some claw back as risks are realized."

Private market players, in other words, are to bear the burden of regulatory failure. They would only receive their compensation after they find out whether governments and regulators have done their jobs and protected against systemic risk. In AIG's case, Mr. Obama is punishing AIG staff for massive, global government failure.

6

The Government Bank Bailout Will Not Jump Start the American Economy

Doug Page

Doug Page is a retired union lawyer and a life-long Democrat. He writes articles for various Internet news services and manages his own blog, the newliberator.com.

American capitalism favors the rich, and now that the system is failing, the rich should be left to their own devices. The government should not hand out bailout money to the bankers and investors that brought about the current financial crisis. Such a move will only reward the risk-takers who, in turn, will likely do nothing to aid the economy. Instead, those unwise speculators should be allowed to go bankrupt, and the bailout money should be used to support healthy banks, build the nation's infrastructure, invest in new energy sources, and give the poor and unemployed assistance so that they can survive the debacle.

Despite all of the talk and promise of hope and change, it is now apparent that President [Barack] Obama plans to try to restart capitalism as it was *prior to August 2007*. He proposes to try to restore the status quo just prior to the present crisis. He also plans to use public funds, our tax money, "as much as is necessary" for this purpose. The total already promised is $7.3 trillion for Wall Street. This is $28,000 of debt for each one of us, our children and grandchildren. If Obama

Doug Page, "The Wall Street Bailout Will Not Jump-start 'Our' Capitalism: Plan B," Dissident Voice, November 29, 2008. Reproduced by permission of www.dissidentvoice.org.

goes ahead with his proposed stimulus package for Main Street, it is estimated that will cost at least $7 trillion more. That will be a debt of $56,000 for each of us. Obama promises to help both Wall Street and Main Street, both the wealthiest 1% and the "middle class," a classification that contains ever diminishing numbers. Those of us who are not a part of the wealthiest 1% are typically economically insecure, worried, poor, and getting poorer in terms of medical care, housing, and even adequate nutritious food, and the new taxes necessary to pay off this tremendous debt. There is an irreconcilable conflict of interest between the top 1%, Wall Street and the very rich, and the bottom 95% consisting of Main Street, the Middle Class, the poor, the homeless and the destitute. Obama now seems to be a servant of Wall Street. We hope that he is a wise prophet with secret future plans, when he promises that we are all united Americans with a common need and a common goal.

Will Obama's efforts, priorities, and huge bailouts rescue Wall Street and the top 1% so that capitalism will be jump started for them and for all of us?

An Economy Saddled with Too Much Debt

President Obama does not now acknowledge how very sick and fragile our capitalism was in August 2007. We were overburdened with credit debt. The economy was kept going by tempting us into more debt by issuing multiple credit cards, and by selling us overpriced subdivision houses with mortgages that we could not afford. As we shall show below, the subprime mess was a natural mutation of the dynamics of our capitalism.

However, most of us continue to give Obama the benefit of the doubt. We have no other choice. We hope and we pray that he, like [Abraham] Lincoln, is making every possible effort to harmonize profoundly conflicting ideologies and levels of wealth, and that he will ultimately do what is right and possible for mankind and fulfill our yearning for hope and healing change. We hope that he will do this without another Civil War, and without the loss of our liberty.

All we can do right now is to raise questions: Will Obama's present plan to give Wall Street $7.3 trillion without effective conditions really stimulate the whole economy? Will Obama's efforts, priorities, and huge bailouts rescue Wall Street and the top 1% so that capitalism will be jump started for them and for all of us?

The Inner Workings of Capitalism Are Problematic

President Obama's selection of University of California Professor Christina Romer as his head economics advisor gives us a hint of what he plans. She, so far as we can tell from her writings, has never studied nor even acknowledged the existence of capitalism's inner dynamics. She seems to assume that capitalism, if left to itself, will work smoothly and permanently with full employment. The insight that we now have as to her interests and beliefs comes from her entry on "Business Cycles" in the Library of Economics and Liberty.

As to the causes of business cycles, recessions and depressions, she writes:

> ... there is no reason why business cycles have to occur at all. The prevailing view among economists is that there is a level of economic activity, often referred to as full employment, at which the economy could stay forever.... If nothing disturbs the economy, the full employment level of output, which naturally tends to grow as the population increases, and newer technologies are discovered, can be maintained forever.

She seems to believe that our capitalism can be controlled simply by tweaking the money supply and the interest rates. If these cycles cause pain among us, she writes: "The advent of unemployment insurance and other social welfare programs means that recessions no longer wreak the havoc on individuals' standard of living that they once did."

In her view of our capitalism: "Everything is grand in Kansas City. Everything is good as it can be."

Although she is said to be a specialist in the causes of the Great Depression, her academic work and writings seem to reflect her interest in simply uncritically and non-judgmentally observing capitalism, and measuring its external movements and tendencies. She assumes capitalism is at least potentially a stable, socially useful system for all of us. She seems to assume that only minor tweaking is needed to keep it going. She does not show interest in the inner workings of capitalism, its tendency toward monopoly, overproduction, and imperialism, in its creation of a tremendous disparity between the rich and the poor and the resulting political power, and its longstanding need for ever increasing public expenditure to avoid economic depression.

The evidence shows that ever since 1980, capitalists could not make a profit producing things that people really need.

She thus assumes a capitalism that has never existed anywhere, at any time. No manipulations of money supply and interest rates have ever made capitalism work with full employment. Born in 1958 and coming of age in 1978, she has never personally experienced or witnessed the pain of the Great Depression. She has apparently not been much influenced by John Steinbeck's book, *The Grapes of Wrath*, whose main character Tom Joad says regarding our capitalism: "There is food to eat and people to eat it, but them two cannot get together. There is work to do and people to do it, but them two cannot get together either." Professor Romer thus deprives herself of much relevant data, insights, and actual experience of the real workings of capitalism during strikes, on the picket line, in the legislative halls, among the victims of industrial pollution, with the sick whose only source of care is the hospital emergency room, and among the homeless, unemployed and underemployed. She apparently has not read Barbara Ehrenreich's book, *Nickel and Dimed*, about a woman's unsuccessful effort to survive in our real economy. She also deprives herself of those who have studied the real inner workings and dynamics of capitalism, or she finds it professionally advantageous to ignore them. (No capitalist business or corporation has ever provided grants to professors or graduate students to study the defects of capitalism.)

The point of all of this is that neither Professor Romer nor President Obama can devise remedies and solutions for the great crisis of our capitalism unless they know the real causes of the crisis.

Every year from 1933 to date, capitalism has needed tremendous contributions of public money to stay out of depression.

A Sick System That Benefits the Rich

Feeding more hay to a sick elephant will only make it sicker if the elephant has cancer in its digestive tract. The evidence shows that our capitalism has "cancer of its metabolism." The evidence shows that ever since 1980, capitalists could not make a profit producing things that people really need. The fact that capitalist employers draw out tremendous salaries and dividends from the production our labor creates and the fact that investment banks draw out more in interest, leaves us employee-consumers with insufficient wages and salaries to buy the goods our labor has produced. So the employers have "overproduction." We still have needs, but there is no profit for capitalists in meeting our needs. They fire us and move on

41

to some other activity where they can make a profit, first overseas in economic imperialism by hiring employees to produce there, at even lower wages.

When even imperialism produced more goods than could be sold, capitalists turned in 1980 to what has been named Financialization. Desperate for new sources of profit, capitalists began to buy and sell each other's companies using the easy credit from investment banks to do so rather than their own accumulated profits or issuing stock. (Interest is tax deductible, while dividends are not.) They also began to invest in subprime mortgages, and then in the many levels of collateralized debt obligations based on these new mortgages. These three or more levels of collateralized debt obligations provided quick Ponzi scheme [fraudulent investment operation] type profit for [former U.S. Secretary of the Treasury and the director of Citigroup] Robert Rubin and his investment banks, but produced absolutely nothing that human beings needed. This is how capitalism actually has worked during recent history. This illustrates the inner dynamics of capitalism. As we see, capitalism was very sick even in 1980 in that there was insufficient profit-making opportunities in producing what people needed. Every year from 1933 to date, capitalism has needed tremendous contributions of public money to stay out of depression. Capitalism has never been robust on its own without public money. It has always been fragile. . . .

It is a pure criminal theft of our money to give $7.3 billion to investment banks, their CEOs and shareholders in the hope that they will again make credit available.

Opening Up More Credit Is Not the Answer

There simply is no credit crisis. There is a demand crisis, a crisis among us voter consumers consisting of our inability to buy what we need. We need more credit like we need a hole in the head. We are already maxed out on credit. The real problem is that people do not earn enough from their labor to buy what capitalism produces. There is an "overproduction" of things that can be sold at a profit, but there simply is not an overproduction of things we really need. So it is a pure criminal theft of our money to give $7.3 billion to investment banks, their CEOs and shareholders in the hope that they will again make credit available. This scandalous gift of public funds is aimed at a problem that does not exist and will do absolutely nothing to solve the problem that does exist. A policy that is aimed at providing profit making opportunities for investment banks on Wall Street will not even produce profit for them. It does absolutely nothing to increase our purchasing power or our earnings or our well being. If we were eagerly ready to pay for more cars and houses, you may be sure that Wall Street banks would find a way to finance them. We are not. We cannot. We have no earned money with which to buy. THAT is the problem. The current strategy involves spending $7.3 trillion in an outright gift to bankrupt, ineptly managed investment banks and insurance companies to relieve them of the liability of now worthless collateralized debt obligations. It is then hoped that they will again extend credit. This is not working, it could work for us if at all only by trickle down, and it cannot work even for Wall Street. Even if the banks are forced to lend money to businesses and credit card holders, there is no way to force anybody or any company to borrow. There is no way this trickle down will create adequate purchasing power among those with needs. It does nothing to solve the inner sickness of capitalism. There is absolutely no reason why we the public should bear the cost of Robert Rubin's stupidity and take over the massive liabilities of the investment banks in these worthless collateralized debt obligations. In order to qualify to invest in those, one had to be a sophisticated wealthy investor. Let Robert Rubin and other investors like him bear the loss of their stupid investments. It is idiotic to let Robert Rubin and his protégés now influence the policy of bailing them out when they are responsible for the problem.

If necessary let our government be the employer and the lender of last resort.

Time for Plan B

With an accurate and realistic analysis of the dynamics of capitalism, one can then fashion pragmatic reforms or substitutes as circumstances demand, a Plan B.

We have plenty of humans willing and anxious to work. We have immense human needs, many of them unmet. We have thousands of businesses ready and willing to meet those needs, although some needs like medical care cannot and should not yield a profit. What is missing is a source of earned purchasing power. Instead, to get things going why not set up a Federal Loan Bank and provide the necessary credit at low interest rates directly to local healthy banks so that they can function normally? These local banks can then meet the routine needs of business for flooring loans, seasonal loans, and other normal long and short term loans. Spend the $7.3 trillion on extending and increasing unemployment benefits, in retraining, building new sources of energy, and rebuilding our bridges and levees. Let's spend it for universal health care. If necessary let our government be the employer and the lender of last resort. Let Robert Rubin's investment banks go bankrupt. Once things are going, we can then consider further steps to solve capitalism's inner sickness. For those human needs that capitalists cannot meet adequately and still make a profit like universal health care, our government can become the employer of last resort. For example, our government can hire doctors, nurses and physician's assistants. It can place a physician's assistant in a drop-in clinic in the corner of drug stores to provide immediate health care. We can then relieve our employers of the expense of providing health care and worker's compensation insured medical care for job injuries.

Our President and our government are so far demonstrating that they are subject to the control of Wall Street.

Let the Investors Go Bankrupt

Since our government is not choosing direct solution, it is apparent that this is a class issue. Wall Street, Robert Rubin and the top 1% naturally prefer that the $7.3 trillion be given to them to compensate them for their stupid investments. We do not need to yield to these outrageous demands. Our President and our government are so far demonstrating that they are subject to the control of Wall Street. Our alternative is to let the investment banks go bankrupt and not us. They created their own problem. There is no sense in letting them take us down with them.

It is also obvious that President Obama, at least for the present, is adopting as his very own, and trying to refuel, the already existing class war of Wall Street and the very rich against the rest of us to convert every minute of our existence into a profit making opportunity. This is obvious from his priority of helping Wall Street first and asking absolutely nothing substantive in return. It is obvious from his support of the Wall Street policy of helping investment banks and insurance companies, but not Ford, Chrysler or GM. The Wall Street policy is to let the auto companies go through bankruptcy to escape their union contracts and health insurance commitments. Wall Street will then help these companies after bankruptcy. The current policy will not work. A Great Depression will soon be upon us. We hope that brilliant, pragmatic, compassionate President Obama and his economic advisor Professor Christina Romer will then stop listening to Robert

Rubin's "solutions." We hope that they will then use our public money to solve the inner sickness of capitalism, and to meet our needs. We will then be truly united Americans with common needs, dreams, and more equal political power.

7

The Government Should Not Bail Out Failing Homeowners

Declan McCullagh

A former reporter for Time *magazine, Declan McCullagh is the chief political correspondent for CNET's News.com. He has also previously served as the Washington, D.C., bureau chief for* Wired News. *His articles have appeared in* The Wall Street Journal, Playboy, *and* The New Republic.

Unwise homebuyers and housing speculators fueled the mortgage crisis that has now left many Americans facing foreclosure. The government plans to step in and aid these risk-takers, but such a bailout scheme only rewards bad behavior. Spending taxpayer money on this plan also punishes those homeowners who did not purchase houses beyond their means. The government needs to rethink this rescue operation in order to bring the concept of responsibility back to home buying.

Perhaps the best argument against a government bailout of underwater homeowners can be found in the character of Casey Serin, a 26-year-old would-be mogul in Sacramento, Calif.

In hopes of getting rich quick, Serin took out $2.2 million in mortgages on eight houses, some sight unseen. He lost all of the properties, most to foreclosure, and says he's recently contemplated living on the streets.

Serin achieved a measure of Internet fame by chronicling his failures at real estate speculation on a now-defunct blog, where an audience of so-called "haterz" spent endless hours critiquing his innumerable financial missteps. After selling his Web site to pay down his then-wife's credit card debt, Serin has had time to reflect on how he and other speculators contributed to the biggest housing bubble in history.

"I personally don't believe in bailouts," Serin said in an interview this week [January 2009]. "If you don't get hurt, what's going to stop you from taking on the risk next time? You're interfering with the natural order of things."

Too bad our elected leaders in Washington, D.C. aren't half as thoughtful as a failed housing speculator.

This is not politically correct to say, but the reality is that not everyone can afford a house.

A Return to Normalcy

The reality is . . . , housing prices leapt too high, too fast, beyond what economic fundamentals permit.

This is why house prices are falling back to earth. Speculators have moved on or, like Serin, are courting bankruptcy. Lending standards are returning to normal. Debt has given way to moderate thrift. The supply of homes exceeds demand in many areas; prices will stabilize only when homes become affordable again and excess inventory is sold.

Unfortunately, our representatives seem unable to let a return to normalcy take place.

Taxpayer aid to prevent foreclosures on mortgages acquired by the government was part of [2008's] last fall's $700 billion bailout. Rep. Barney Frank, a Massachusetts Democrat, now wants that money to be used to rewrite mortgages and reduce monthly payments. Politicians are being egged on by homebuilders, real estate agents and lumber companies that set up FixHousingFirst.com, a Web site urging taxpayer-funded "foreclosure prevention" and "discounted mortgage financing" to "increase home values."

That's a little like propping up Pets.com shares during their post-dot com bubble slide toward 19 cents and eventual liquidation.

Aiding the Undeserving

No matter what Washington promises, homeowner bailouts will aid the undeserving—the Casey Serins and speculators of his ilk—at the expense of the fiscally prudent. Why should Americans who rented and saved their pennies for a 20 percent down payment be taxed to bail out those who gambled and lost? Where in the U.S. Constitution has Congress been delegated the power to hand out such largesse? And do banks and lenders need government help to decide whether writing down loans is better than expensive foreclosures?

This is not politically correct to say, but the reality is that not everyone can afford a house. A fast food assistant manager makes $9.95 an hour, and the median price of a new home sold last fall was around $218,400. With reasonable assumptions about taxes and interest rates, our assistant manager would have $0 a month left over for food, clothing, and car payments. Unless a house is unusually cheap, renting could be wiser.

Yet for at least a decade, the official policy of the U.S. government has been that if you breathe, you qualify for a mortgage. As George Mason University economics professor Russell Roberts noted, that official policy is what created the housing bubble—nonexistent oversight of Fannie and Freddie [i.e., Fannie Mae (Federal National Mortgage Association) and Freddie Mac (Federal Home Loan Mortgage Corporation), the two government-supported mortgage lenders]; the Federal Reserve's artificially low interest rates; the Community Reinvestment Act and its [Bill] Clinton-era expansion; and a 1997 law that made capital gains tax-free.

Uncle Sam's Blessing

In June 2002, President [George W.] Bush announced "America's Homeownership Challenge" that included $200 million annually for down payment assistance, and $2.4 billion for homes to be sold to low and moderate income families. A year later, Bush proclaimed National Homeownership Month by saying "American values of individuality, thrift, responsibility and self-reliance are embodied in homeownership." (A cranky Barney Frank responded by claiming Bush hadn't gone far enough.)

We know how that turned out. Americans queued up for exotic zero-down mortgages on houses they couldn't afford, with unscrupulous lenders taking advantage of greedy buyers, all with Uncle Sam's blessing. Then came foreclosures and trashed credit and realization that many buyers would have been better off renting all along. (The average home ownership rate from 1970 to 1990 was 64 percent, according to U.S. Census data. Today the rate remains at a historically high figure of 68 percent.)

"Pain is one of the best ways to make change happen," said Serin, the speculator-turned-tell-all-blogger. "If you were just completely reckless about it, you deserve to fall flat on your face. I was reckless. But I don't know what I deserve."

One thing Serin doesn't deserve is a taxpayer bailout. Alas, if Rep. Frank and his political allies have their way with our pocketbooks, others who were just as irresponsible and dishonest will receive precisely that.

8

The Bank Bailout Neglects Responsible Homeowners

Nancy Rapoport

Nancy Rapoport is the Gordon & Silver Professor of Law at the William S. Boyd School of Law at the University of Nevada in Las Vegas. She is an expert in bankruptcy, corporate governance, and business ethics. She is the coauthor of Enron: Corporate Fiascos and Their Implications.

The mortgage bailout is aimed at those Americans who bought homes they could not afford. It will not do anything to help those financially responsible homeowners who pay their mortgages and yet have suffered a loss of value in their own homes as the markets collapsed. This latter group of individuals could use assistance as well, especially because it is their money that the government hopes will help rebuild the economy. But these responsible debt payers will be overlooked as the government focuses on—and rewards—those bad risk takers that contributed to the mortgage crisis.

I have a lot of sympathy for those who are caught in the middle of the mortgage crisis—more sympathy than you might realize. And, like many of us, I hope that the stimulus package actually does some good for our economy, although I doubt that there are any clear answers about how to fix an economy that's gone horribly wrong. (Yes, some of the best minds in the country are working on this problem—both inside and outside the administration; but the best that they can do is make educated guesses about what the best fixes will be.) So far, what we know about the "mortgage fixes" announced Wednesday [February 18, 2009] is that it focuses on two sectors of distressed homeowners: those who are already in default and those who are teetering on the edge of default.

There is, however, a group that has been excluded from every one of the proposed rescues: those homeowners who took out very boring (30-year fixed) mortgages on houses whose values have plummeted. These homeowners sound a lot like the ones about whom Congress and the President [Barack Obama] are worrying, but there's a key difference: the excluded group isn't in danger of default, has not stopped paying its bills (including its mortgages), and will not be rescued by any of the proposals to date.

What of the homeowners who came up with those down-payments, demonstrated their credit-worthiness?

No Bailout for Responsible Homeowners

The news loves to cover those people who took out interest-only mortgages, those who took out adjustable-rate mortgages where the first interest rate jump created a monthly mortgage bill that far exceeded the homeowner's [ability] to pay, or those who bought several houses as investment properties, or my favorite—the NINJA mortgage (given to a borrower with no verifiable income, job, or assets). There's plenty of blame to go around: banks that may not have disclosed exactly how tricky these mortgage terms were; borrowers who bought much more house than they could afford; rating agencies that bought—hook, line, and sinker—the claim that securities based on risky loans would not carry a significant risk of default.

But what of the banks that required down payments in the 15–20% range, used conventional, fixed-rate mortgages and 15- to 30-year terms, and verified all of the borrowers' financial information before agreeing to lend the money? And what of the homeowners who came up with those down payments, demonstrated their credit-worthiness, and—here is the key—continue to hold jobs that allow them to pay their mortgages each month? Their homes very likely are just as underwater as the homes down the block (the ones with the riskiest mortgages), but no one's talking about restructuring their mortgages. The discussion of modifying the Bankruptcy Code to allow stripdown of first mortgages in chapter 13 cases won't apply to this group, which doesn't plan to file for bankruptcy protection at all.

My guess is that many of the people [who pay their mortgage debts] feel a bit like chumps.

How the Debt Payers Lose Out

It's an interesting group, this forgotten segment. It's made of people who know that their mortgage payments aren't going to rebuild equity in their homes any time soon, because the value of their homes is too far gone to allow for equity in the foreseeable future. It's made of people who see the "for sale" and "foreclosure" signs in their neighborhoods and who have read about "jingle mail" (mailing the keys to the bank and just walking away from their homes entirely).

My guess is that many of the people in this group feel a bit like chumps: they're honoring their debts, at significant cost, because they are people who pay their debts if they possibly can—even though walking away would be a lot easier. (To be sure, this group is made of people with good credit scores who don't want to see those scores ruined by a foreclosure or a bankruptcy.)

This group is also key to the country's stimulus: with jobs and assets, this group can still spend money, which—if you believe the experts—is a good thing to infuse into our economy.

But what one thing can't this group do? It can't refinance its homes to take advantage of any new lower interest rates or any new tax breaks. Why? Because this group—like the borrowers with the risky mortgages—has no equity in its homes and, in all likelihood, no ability to find another 15–20% down as part of the refinancing. Take a simple example: my own situation. Eighteen months ago, we bought a house for $380,000 and put approximately 15% down. As of today, our home is worth $267,500, according to Zillow.com, so there's no more equity in the house. (Our home's value went down because other homes in our neighborhood are either going unsold or are foreclosed properties.) It's possible that mortgage rates will go down as a result of the stimulus package, but we won't be able to take advantage of any refinancing. The proposal itself only targets people whose outstanding mortgage balance doesn't exceed 105% of the home's value (for us, that would be $280,875 in home value, with just a hair over $300,000 still owed, so we don't qualify). Because we're part of the group not covered by the plan, and because there's no equity left in the house to give a bank any incentive to give us a new mortgage—and, most important, because we're not defaulting on any payments—there's no incentive to bring our bank to the table to restructure our loan. Why should our bank renegotiate? We're paying our bills, and we have our jobs—we're just underwater. Congress hasn't said one word about forcing banks to take care of folks like us, and I doubt that it will (or that it can).

Reward Bad Risk Takers

Our group isn't super-rich (or even moderately rich), so there is a very real cost to us of having lost all of the equity in our homes. From everything I've read, our group will be worse off over time than the groups who are getting bailed out. Where's the bailout for people like us—people who did the right thing and bought the amount of house that they could afford, only to find out that all of the risks that other people took has destroyed the value of their homes, too?

Until the bailout takes care of my group, it's not really a bailout at all: it's a reward for extreme risk-taking behavior—behavior that went beyond the bounds of common sense. And what lessons get learned when you reward bad risk-taking behavior? That bad risks are really quite good risks, in the end.

9

The Government Should Nationalize Banks

Matthew Rothschild

Matthew Rothschild is the editor of The Progressive, *a liberal newsmagazine focused on American politics and culture. He is the author of* You Have No Rights: Stories of America in an Age of Repression. *Rothschild is also the co-founder and director of The Progressive Media Project, which distributes opinion pieces to newspapers around the country in an effort to democratize and diversify the range of viewpoints offered to the American public.*

The financial crisis has shown that banks have little regard for public interest and are simply concerned with saving their private shareholders. Because of this, the government bailout money has remained locked up in the banks and has not induced the private owners to begin lending again. To rectify this problem, the government should have bought the banks outright and converted them to public institutions, guaranteeing that they would start lending out money in order to speed an overall economic recovery.

One Treasury official after another is doing somersaults on a wire to distract us from the obvious: We need to nationalize many of the banks, not save them as private entities.

The banks got us into this financial mess in the first place by making unwise home loans and by speculating in unregulated credit-default swaps tied to those loans. They have taken the entire world economy down with them. They don't deserve to be bailed out.

If our government really believed in free enterprise, these banks would be out of business right now.

Instead, first the [George W.] Bush Administration and now the [Barack] Obama Administration have decided to act like an iron lung for the banks, pumping hundreds of billions of dollars into them to keep them alive.

There is no reason to do that.

And it would have been cheaper to buy them outright.

The Banks Have Already Been Bought

"The day we gave Citigroup their second infusion we could have bought them for the same $20 billion," says economist Dean Baker. "On top of that, we guaranteed $300 billion of assets. We could have bought Citigroup several times over."

Still, the banks aren't solvent. Baker estimates that the losses on most of their balance sheets outweigh their capital. This is a recipe for indefinite bailouts.

If we're the major shareholders, as we now are with Citigroup and Bank of America, we ought to have a major say [in how banks are run].

Nobel Prize-winner in economics Joseph Stiglitz also sees the irrationality of leaving the banks in private hands.

"In effect, the American taxpayers are the major provider of finance to the banks," he wrote on CNN's website. "In some cases, the value of our equity injection, guarantees, and other forms of assistance dwarfs the value of the 'private' sector's equity contribution. Yet we have no voice in how the banks are run."

We don't have a voice because the Bush Administration tied no strings to the $350 billion. But if we're the major shareholders, as we now are with Citigroup (taxpayers hold a 7.8 percent stake) and Bank of America (6 percent), we ought to have a major say. And if we're going to throw more money at them, why not just purchase the banks themselves?

If we want companies to receive loans, why not get rid of the middleman, and have the government lend directly to businesses and to homeowners?

Hoarding the Cash

The banks have not done what the government told us they were supposed to do when it lavished the first $350 billion on them. They didn't start lending more. "The last thing in their mind was to restart lending," wrote Stiglitz. And even today, they have a strong incentive to sit on their cash.

"There is still no assurance of a resumption of lending," Stiglitz explains. "Having been burned once, many bankers are staying away from the fire. . . . Many a bank may decide that the better strategy is a conservative one: Hoard one's cash, wait until things settle down, hope that you are among the few surviving banks, and then start lending. Of course, if all the banks reason so, the recession will be longer and deeper than it otherwise would be."

So, since lending is vital to the economy, and since the private banks won't lend, let's buy up some insolvent banks so we can get the lending going ourselves. The private sector has proven that it can't or won't do the job. The public sector must step in. Put a different way, if we want companies to receive loans, why not get rid of the middleman, and have the government lend directly to businesses and to homeowners?

"For the moment, there's no choice," says Robert Pollin, professor of economics at the University of Massachusetts-Amherst. "Relative to a year ago, lending in the U.S. economy is down an astonishing 90 percent. The government needs to take over the banks now, and force them to start lending." (Pollin wants the government to sell the banks back into private hands, later on, with stringent regulations.)

We're shelling out gobs of public money for these [banks] ... but we're not running these companies in the public interest.

Private Companies Do Not Operate for Public Interest

Truly nationalized banks, run by the government for the people, would help out the economy as a whole. As Stiglitz put it, under private ownership, there's a "huge gap between private rewards and social returns." Under public ownership, "the incentives of the banks can be aligned better with those of the country. And it is in the national interest that prudent lending be restarted."

We could reap other social returns from nationalization, as well. "If the banks were nationalized, the government could declare a moratorium on foreclosures for the properties it controls, and move to restructure mortgages—perhaps at subsidized rates—for homeowners," writes Joshua Holland of AlterNet.

As it is right now, we're getting some of the vices of nationalization without all the virtues. We're shelling out gobs of public money for these companies—in many cases, more money than the companies are actually worth—but we're not running these companies in the public interest. We're allowing the companies to remain in private hands, for private purposes.

"We have a financial system that is run by private shareholders, managed by private institutions, and we'd like to do our best to preserve that system," said Treasury Secretary Timothy Geithner.

Why is that the job of the Obama Administration?

I thought its job was to make the economy work for the American public. And keeping the banks in private hands isn't getting the job done. Throwing hundreds of billions of dollars, over and over, to keep these banks on life support makes no sense.

Unless you want to ensure that the shareholders get artificially inflated returns and the executives get to keep their jobs.

Or unless you are too snug in your ideological straitjacket to even consider the most rational way to proceed.

Fears about Nationalization

And that's the problem today. The word "nationalization" shuts off the debate. Never mind that Britain, facing the same crisis we are, just nationalized the Bank of Scotland. Never mind that [President] Ronald Reagan himself considered such an option during a global banking crisis in the early 1980s.

"When a bank is insolvent, the regulators put it into receivership," says James Galbraith, professor of government at the LBJ [Lyndon Baines Johnson] School of Public Affairs of the University of Texas at Austin. "The Reagan Administration had a plan to do it with all the big banks in 1982 and 1983, if a single large Latin American country had defaulted. Let me repeat that: the Reagan Administration."

But the Obama Administration is not considering receivership, much less genuine nationalization in the interests of the majority of Americans. Cluttered with worshippers of the private sector, skittish about being tagged "leftist," and beset by obdurate Republicans, the Obama Administration has blocked off the path to true nationalization. Instead, it is opting for gimmicky proposals to take some bad debts off the books—all in service of those "private shareholders" that Geithner so adores.

Granted, nationalization over the long haul is a risky business, too, which is why Pollin resists it.

"We would have every reason to expect a wide range of failures and misjudgments, including 'crony capitalism'— privileged back-room dealings with selected non-financial firms," Pollin writes in *Boston Review*.

Pollin is also worried about the political fallout. "The failures of the nationalized system could be the very thing— perhaps the only thing—that could shift the target of public outrage over the collapse of the financial system off Wall Street and onto the U.S. government," he wrote.

While these are certainly legitimate concerns, we've seen what the private sector does—not only when left to its own devices but also when bailed out by hundreds of billions of our funds.

Yes, if it took over some of the banks, the government would have to carefully design a system to prevent corruption. And yes, there would be bumps along the road.

But we've had enough bumps on the road marked "private."

If we're going to be shelling out the money, we might as well run the store.

10

The Government Should Temporarily Nationalize Banks

Paul Krugman

Paul Krugman is a professor of economics and international affairs at Princeton University. He is a frequent op-ed columnist for the New York Times. *In 2008, Krugman was awarded the Nobel Prize in Economic Science.*

Because America's banks are near failure and need to be rescued, the government should step in and nationalize these institutions. After all, the government has already promised to bail out the banks with more money than their current asset value. It would be simpler, then, to buy the banks and get them back to financial soundness. Once that is accomplished, the government could restore these institutions to private ownership.

Comrade Greenspan wants us to seize the economy's commanding heights.

O.K., not exactly. What Alan Greenspan, the former Federal Reserve chairman—and a staunch defender of free markets—actually said was, "It may be necessary to temporarily nationalize some banks in order to facilitate a swift and orderly restructuring." I agree.

The case for nationalization rests on three observations.

First, some major banks are dangerously close to the edge—in fact, they would have failed already if investors didn't expect the government to rescue them if necessary.

Paul Krugman, "Banking on the Brink," *The New York Times*, February 23, 2009, p. 27.

Second, banks must be rescued. The collapse of Lehman Brothers almost destroyed the world financial system, and we can't risk letting much bigger institutions like Citigroup [Citi] or Bank of America [BofA] implode.

Third, while banks must be rescued, the U.S. government can't afford, fiscally or politically, to bestow huge gifts on bank shareholders.

Let's be concrete here. There's a reasonable chance—not a certainty—that Citi and BofA, together, will lose hundreds of billions over the next few years. And their capital, the excess of their assets over their liabilities, isn't remotely large enough to cover those potential losses.

The Rise of Zombie Banks

Arguably, the only reason they haven't already failed is that the government is acting as a backstop, implicitly guaranteeing their obligations. But they're zombie banks, unable to supply the credit the economy needs.

The funds needed to bring these banks fully back to life would greatly exceed what they're currently worth.

To end their zombiehood the banks need more capital. But they can't raise more capital from private investors. So the government has to supply the necessary funds.

But here's the thing: the funds needed to bring these banks fully back to life would greatly exceed what they're currently worth. Citi and BofA have a combined market value of less than $30 billion, and even that value is mainly if not entirely based on the hope that stockholders will get a piece of a government handout. And if it's basically putting up all the money, the government should get ownership in return.

America Already Utilizes Nationalization Strategies

Still, isn't nationalization un-American? No, it's as American as apple pie.

Lately the Federal Deposit Insurance Corporation [F.D.I.C.] has been seizing banks it deems insolvent at the rate of about two a week. When the F.D.I.C. seizes a bank, it takes over the bank's bad assets, pays off some of its debt, and resells the cleaned-up institution to private investors. And that's exactly what advocates of temporary nationalization want to see happen, not just to the small banks the F.D.I.C. has been seizing, but to major banks that are similarly insolvent.

Tepid Government Bailout Plans

The real question is why the [Barack] Obama administration keeps coming up with proposals that sound like possible alternatives to nationalization, but turn out to involve huge handouts to bank stockholders.

For example, the administration initially floated the idea of offering banks guarantees against losses on troubled assets. This would have been a great deal for bank stockholders, not so much for the rest of us: heads they win, tails taxpayers lose.

The longer we live with zombie banks, the harder it will be to end the economic crisis.

Now the administration is talking about a "public-private partnership" to buy troubled assets from the banks, with the government lending money to private investors for that purpose. This would offer investors a one-way bet: if the assets rise in price, investors win; if they fall substantially, investors walk away and leave the government holding the bag. Again, heads they win, tails we lose.

Why not just go ahead and nationalize? Remember, the longer we live with zombie banks, the harder it will be to end the economic crisis.

Long-Term Government Ownership Is Not the Goal

How would nationalization take place? All the administration has to do is take its own planned "stress test" for major banks seriously, and not hide the results when a bank fails the test, making a takeover necessary. Yes, the whole thing would have a Claude Rains feel to it, as a government that has been propping up banks for months declares itself shocked, shocked at the miserable state of their balance sheets.[1] But that's O.K.

And once again, long-term government ownership isn't the goal: like the small banks seized by the F.D.I.C. every week, major banks would be returned to private control as soon as possible. The finance blog Calculated Risk suggests that instead of calling the process nationalization, we should call it "preprivatization."

The Obama administration, says Robert Gibbs, the White House spokesman, believes "that a privately held banking system is the correct way to go." So do we all. But what we have now isn't private enterprise, it's lemon socialism: banks get the upside but taxpayers bear the risks. And it's perpetuating zombie banks, blocking economic recovery.

What we want is a system in which banks own the downs as well as the ups. And the road to that system runs through nationalization.

---

1. In the film *Casablanca*, Claude Rains's character, a policeman aware of illegal activity, pretends to be shocked by it when it is discovered by his superiors.

11

The Government Should Not Nationalize Banks

Rick Newman

Rick Newman is the chief business correspondent for U.S. News & World Report. *He is the author of* Firefight: Inside the Battle to Save the Pentagon on 9/11 *and* Bury Us Upside Down: The Misty Pilots and the Secret Battle for the Ho Chi Minh Trail.

Despite the gravity of the financial crisis, any plan to nationalize banks as a corrective response would be wrongheaded. Government control of banks would not cover all the losses accrued, and it would simply depress the value of the remaining stockholders' shares. Nationalization might also cause further panic and affect the stability of healthy banks, widening the scale of the problem.

Scan the headlines, and you'd think it's a no-brainer: The government takes over the most troubled banks, whips them back into shape, then returns them to the private sector in a few years. Problem solved.

Former Federal Reserve Chairman Alan Greenspan has advocated nationalizing select banks. Famed prognosticator Nouriel Roubini says it's the only way to go, since the whole sector is effectively insolvent. Sen. Chris Dodd, chairman of the Senate Banking Committee, roiled the markets recently by saying nationalization may be necessary for awhile.

A federal takeover of Citigroup [Citi], Bank of America, and other tottering giants might end up being the only logical thing to do. But nationalizing such banks would be a desperate move, with no guarantee that it would accomplish anything the banks can't do for themselves.

Worst of all, a dramatic federal takeover might create expectations that the government can solve a deeply vexing problem overnight—then leave the nation feeling more distressed than ever when the move fails to stem vast losses, revive the credit markets or fix the foreclosure epidemic. Here's why nationalizing the banks would be so draconian:

It wouldn't solve the underlying problem. The main problem at struggling banks like Citigroup is a mountain of losses—which the banks may not have enough cash to cover. Those losses are already a done deal: They stem from mounting defaults on loans given to homeowners over the last several years, and also to car buyers, students paying for college, and consumers who ran up credit-card balances they can't pay off. The banks have written off some of those losses. But many still lurk, since the deepening recession means more people will lose their jobs and the ability to pay their bills.

Nationalizing [troubled] banks would be a desperate move, with no guarantee that it would accomplish anything the banks can't do for themselves.

The government can pump taxpayer dollars into banks to help cover losses, which it's already doing. But even if it owns the banks, "the government can't make embedded losses go away," says economist James Barth of the nonprofit Milken Institute. "The question is how to prevent additional losses." If troubled banks were making wild decisions that were exacerbating their problems, then a government takeover might be one way to install more prudent management. But by most accounts, government regulators are now watching troubled banks so carefully that they're effectively clamping down on any risky moves anyway. So it's not clear what additional protection nationalization would add.

If the government took over a bank, public shares would suddenly be worthless and shareholders would lose everything.

A government takeover would vaporize a lot of wealth. This is why the markets freak out every time there's a rumor, or a rumor of a rumor, about nationalization. If the government took over a bank, public shares would suddenly be worthless and shareholders would lose everything. With Citi and Bank of America shares down more than 90 percent over the last 12 months, many shareholders have already lost a fortune. But there's still a chance they'll get some of it back if the bank recovers. That potential upside would disappear if the feds stepped in.

Even worse, the banks' bondholders and other creditors could lose a bundle too. Same with depositors and institutional customers whose account balances exceed the amount guaranteed by the FDIC [Federal Deposit Insurance Corporation]. To prevent a panic, the government would probably cover those stakeholders up to a certain level—with taxpayers footing the bill once again.

There are thorny geopolitical questions. One of Citigroup's biggest shareholders, for instance, is Saudi Prince Alwaleed bin Talal. You might not shed tears if a Saudi billionaire lost a bunch of money when his Citi shares got wiped out. But last year, Alwaleed was lauded as a white knight when he increased his stake in Citi, while other financiers were sitting on their money and staying out of sight. Plenty of other foreign investors—including sovereign wealth funds run by national governments—hold big stakes in U.S. banks. Like it or not, banks today require investors from all over the world. Wiping out foreign investments could easily scare away money that banks need to survive.

Wiping out foreign investments could easily scare away money that banks need to survive.

Nationalization could easily incite a panic. If the government takes over one or two banks, the obvious question is how many more are in equally desperate shape. Shares in the entire banking sector would plummet even more than they have already. Short sellers, capitalizing on the panic, would drive shares even lower. The government could make a definitive statement limiting its acquisitions to a fixed number of banks, and no more. But to do that, it would have to know for sure that losses at other banks wouldn't become equally insurmountable. And that's the very thing nobody knows, since it depends on the depth of the recession and other factors that are far beyond anybody's control at this point. If the feds nationalized a few banks, said they were done, and then found it necessary to nationalize a few more, that would look absolutely desperate and send the markets into a paroxysm [sudden fit of violent action].

Somebody would still have to run the banks. A key reason for the government to take over a bank would be to boot the existing management. That might sound satisfying, but it raises all sorts of troubling questions. "Who's going to replace current management?" asks Barth. "Some assistant secretary of the Treasury? Does President [Barack] Obama become chairman of the board? Would they run it like the U.S. Postal System? Would that instill more confidence in the banking sector, or less?"

Besides, many of the CEOs who caused the worst problems at firms like Citi, Merrill Lynch, Wachovia, Washington Mutual and Countrywide Financial are long gone. Most of the people now running those banks, or the remnants of them, are cleaning up problems left by others.

Nationalization could threaten healthy banks. If Citigroup were run by the government, it would suddenly be the safest bank in the country. If you had a big account at a private bank that seemed a little less safe, what would you do? Leave your money there? Or transfer it over to the government bank? If healthy banks started losing customers, that would make existing problems even worse.

If healthy banks started losing customers, that would make existing problems even worse.

The banks might recover on their own. There's no doubt it's going to be a tense year for banks, and there will be more failures. But the banks will recover when the economy does. Propping them up until then will require profound patience and probably a lot more money. But that may be a lot better than the alternative.

12

The Government Should Not Bail Out the Auto Industry

Jon Christian Ryter

Jon Christian Ryter is the pseudonym of a former newspaper reporter with the Parkersburg, W.V., Sentinel. He authored a syndicated newspaper column, "Answers from the Bible," from the mid-1970s until 1985. Today he is an advertising executive with the Washington Times.

The U.S. taxpayer should not be expected to bail out the failing auto industry. The Big Three automakers—Ford, General Motors, and Chrysler—have foolishly spent the past decade building gas-guzzling trucks and sport utility vehicles while smart foreign competitors have tooled their fleets to meet the needs of price-conscious consumers. As the economy has soured, Detroit automakers have laid off workers and sent much of the industry overseas instead of matching their product to the economic climate. Americans should feel no sympathy for such poorly managed corporations, and the government should not provide rescue packages to the automakers unless they agree to return outsourced jobs to the United States.

Socialist President-elect Barack Hussein Obama campaigned on message of "change," promising the downtrodden masses that he would be their Robin Hood—taking from the rich and giving to the working class. Instead, he has torn another page from the FDR [Franklin Delano Roosevelt] playbook and is about to reincarnate sitting president George W. Bush into a 21st century Herbert Hoover [whom many blamed for the Great Depression], letting Bush take the blame for bailing out Detroit before he leaves office. This will allow Obama to take the socialist high ground and rail against Big Business Republicans, further damaging the GOP's [Republican party's] chances of regaining seats in the midterm election of 2010.

Bush will try to cut a deal with Obama to save some of his executive decisions that he knows Obama will negate on January 20, 2009 during his first hour as the 44th President of the United States. Even though both Bush and Obama live in the world of the super elite where handshakes are more binding than signed contracts, the current president should realize that Obama is a consummate liar whose word is not his bond. Regardless what promises are made between the two in the sanctity and secrecy of the Oval Office, Obama will not keep any promises that contravene the agenda he has planned for the first 100 days of his administration.

The Mortgage Crisis Coverup

Obama, let Sen. John McCain [of Arizona] take the blame for the financial crisis that started with Obama's street advocacy in Chicago in 1992 when he strong-armed local banks to provide risky loans to minorities, threatening to brand the bankers as racists if they did not. Obama, as both a State Senator [in Illinois] and a US Senator, worked with Fannie Mae [Federal National Mortgage Association, a government-supported mortgage lender] executives to guarantee what would become known as "subprime loans," creating an industry that both the [Bill] Clinton and Bush-43 [George W. Bush, 43rd President] Administrations latched onto in desperation as the US jobs-exports "industry" went into full swing as Detroit moved their plants from the American continent to China. Construction, not factory work, became the number one industry in the

United States. Home construction created jobs. But newly-constructed homes needed to be sold.

It can honestly be said that Barack Hussein Obama, who strong-armed Illinois banks to provide risky mortgage loans to minority buyers who lacked credit standing, was instrumental in creating the subprime mortgage industry. The loans generated by Obama's street advocacy in the early 1990s were backed by Fannie Mae. Obama's advocacy in Illinois became the model for the subprime mortgage industry that was jump-started by Bill Clinton and continued, to its demise, under George W. Bush who ultimately got the blame for its collapse. The pitfall—loaning money to people with credit histories that show they will default on their loans—was concealed by the Congressional Black Caucus and the Democratic leadership which actually believes that people who refuse to work should be granted economic equality paid for by sweat equity of those who slave to provide a better life for their families.

The Democratic congressional leadership quietly met with Detroit automakers and agreed to funnel $25 billion of the $700 billion taxpayer-financed bank bailout to GM.

The Auto Industry Cries Wolf

On the top end of the handout scale, while Congress ... was on "election recess," the Democratic congressional leadership quietly met with Detroit automakers and agreed to funnel $25 billion of the $700 billion taxpayer-financed bank bailout to GM as General Motors stock plummeted to $3.36 per share.

Once the world's largest automaker, GM executives told House Speaker Nancy Pelosi [D-CA], House Majority Leader Steny Hoyer [D-MD], Fred Upton [R-MI], co-chairman of the Congressional Auto Caucus (the token Republican to make it a bipartisan effort) and other senior Democrats that they were going to have to lay off 5,500 workers almost immediately because the automaker said it feared they would run out of cash before the end of the year. (The bailout would give GM over $4.5 million per job saved.) And, to make the prospects even more dismal, GM warned that GM's ". . . future path is likely to be bankruptcy-like." (Perhaps GM could borrow from DiTech, their wholly-owned, cash-flush mortgage finance company.)

When GM cried wolf the first and second time, they had over $50 billion in cash reserves.

Even with the impassioned pleas of the Speaker of the House and Senate Majority Leader Harry Reid [D-NV] begging Bush to include the automakers in the Treasury's bailout program (which was conceived and enacted into law to stabilize banks which had gotten badly burned from the subprime mortgage business they were forced, by law, to underwrite), the Bush-43 Administration has resisted calls from the Democratic leadership to further indulge Ford, GM, and Chrysler. Bush-43 officials reminded the Democratic leadership that Detroit already received $25 billion in low-interest loans to "jump-start" the auto industry. What Bush should have given them was booster cables and a battery charger. (If you recall, GM and Ford both cried wolf in 2005 and again in 2006 because their profits slipped. GM claimed to have lost $10 billion because of rising healthcare costs. Screaming mass layouts both automakers got top union officials to agree to wage cuts for current employees and both jettisoned healthcare coverage for retirees. When Vegas casino magnate Kirk Kerkorian bought 10% of GM's stock he commented that GM CEO Rick Wagoner had done a ". . . great job warehousing cash." When GM cried wolf the first and second time, they had over $50 billion in cash reserves.

An Un-American Industry

That aside, let me pose a question. What would be your prospects of getting a loan from your friendly neighborhood bank if you walked in and told them you needed a loan because it was likely you were going to go bankrupt next year? I mean, if banks were still actually in the business of loaning money to ordinary citizens. Silly me. Instead of jump-starting the economy with that $700 billion, the bailout money is being used by solvent banks to buy insolvent banks and get tax write-offs that exceed the prices they paid for the failing banks. But then, back to my original question. The answer? Zero. Zip. Nada.

In an era of rising gas prices, Ford, GM and Chrysler failed to read the proverbial tea leaves.

Let's take off the rose-colored glasses and look at this picture in stunning black and white. The US auto industry is failing because ... well, it's no longer the US auto industry. It likes to call itself the American auto industry because it's an all-encompassing hemispheric "American" entity. The Big-3 has plants in Canada, Mexico and now, in South America. They claim their cars are all "American-made" when they are showcased in US dealerships because, being transnationalists, they no longer distinguish between the United States, Mexico and Canada—or Brazil and Argentina.

The world has become their global smorgasbord.

In an era of rising gas prices, Ford, GM and Chrysler failed to read the proverbial tea leaves. Failing to take a lesson from history when vehicle downsizing during the gas crisis of the 1970s was the economic rule of thumb, Detroit (a [euphemism] for the auto industry even though almost no cars are made in the Motor City), did the opposite. It not only continued to build gas guzzling monster trucks and SUVs, it even made them bigger. As much as 80% of the inventories of

Ford, GM and Dodge were extended cab pickup trucks and oversized SUVs. If you wanted a traditional passenger car without waiting six weeks for delivery you bought a Toyota, a Honda or a Hyundai—all of which are more "American" than the American car sitting in your driveway if that car was made in 1999 or later. In 2006 there were 7.6 million motor vehicles sold in the United States. Of those, 5.5 million—including Ford, Chrysler and GM—were imported under NAFTA [North American Free Trade Agreement] regulations. What that means is that only 2.1 million of the vehicles that were purchased by US consumers were actually built in the United States by US labor. And, about 75% of those domestic cars and trucks were actually Japanese or Korean branded vehicles: Toyota, Honda and Hyundai.

A Quid Pro Quo Offer

So here's the $25 billion question. Why in the world should the US taxpayers bail out Detroit? There are virtually no jobs at stake because there are virtually no Ford, Chrysler or GM passenger cars or trucks made in the United States. If the Big-3 need a quick fix from government, they need to ask Beijing, Ottawa, Mexico City, Buenos Aires or Brasilia. If the governors in the states where what few Big-3 vehicles are built want to kick in state money to make Detroit's financial statements look better for investors by erasing the losses that stupid auto designers who decided to upsize their vehicles when the world was downsizing, caused, so be it. Those governors can answer to the voters in their states.

If the Big-3 need a quick fix from government, they need to ask Beijing, Ottawa, Mexico City, Buenos Aires or Brasilia.

However, the American people—i.e., US citizens—should not be expected to bail out international companies who, collectively, have more money than those collective taxpayers. Unless, of course, there is a quid pro quo for the taxpayers. What quid pro quo? If GM wants a $25 billion bailout, here's the price: close down all manufacturing plants in China, Mexico, and Brazil and return those jobs to the United States. The same goes for Ford and Chrysler. Jobs for money. It sounds like a good idea to me.

13

The Government Should Bail Out the Auto Industry

Brett Hoven, Katie Quarles, and Tony Wilsdon

Brett Hoven is an auto worker in Minneapolis. He has written several articles for the Socialist Alternative Web site as well as other labor news media. Katie Quarles and Tony Wilsdon also write for the Socialist Alternative.

The crisis in the auto industry has been years in the making. It has been brought about by shortsighted executives trying to maximize profits without taking into account the long-term health of the industry. By building fuel-inefficient vehicles, management has shown that it is not in tune with the public's economic and environmental concerns. In addition, the unions have abetted management's goals and failed to fight to redirect the industry. To resolve the crisis, the government should bail out the industry but then take the opportunity to eliminate corporate ownership and transform the auto giants into public entities run by workers and elected representatives. Once the industry is democratized, it will quickly respond to consumer interests and environmental pressures, which will ensure a long life for America's auto trade.

The Big Three auto companies [Ford, General Motors (GM), and Chrysler] and the United Auto Workers (UAW) are lobbying Congress for $25 billion. The Democrats and the incoming [Barack] Obama administration say they want to negotiate this.

Brett Hoven, Katie Quarles, and Tony Wilsdon, "Billions to Bail Out Banks— Not a Penny for Auto Workers—Defend Jobs through Public Ownership," Socialist Alternative.org, November 26, 2008. Reproduced by permission.

The auto industry which employs 3 million Americans in auto plants, parts factories, and dealerships nationwide, affects over 10 million people when their families are included. If it's allowed to go bankrupt or collapse, which some commentators now consider as a serious possibility, it would devastate the lives of workers, retirees, and communities across the country. Its effects would be most immediate in Michigan, Ohio, and Indiana.

At a time when the government is almost daily stepping in to pledge tens of billions of dollars to bail out giant banks like Citibank for their criminal financial practices, politicians have failed to provide $25 billion to restore a viable auto industry.

GM ... announced that they were burning through billions in cash reserves each month and would be bankrupt in the first half of 2009. Ford and Chrysler are reportedly not far behind.

A Crisis Many Years in the Making

The big questions to be decided are: Will this be another bailout to the owners, managers and CEOs of an industry that they have run into the ground? Or, will the funds be directed to drastically overhaul the products coming out of Detroit, and create a new environmentally-friendly transportation industry for the future, while protecting living wage jobs and providing job security for the existing workforce?

It's clear the automotive industry is facing a massive crisis. October [2008] sales for Ford fell by 30%. At GM sales fell a whopping 45%, making October GM's worst sales month since 1979. GM also announced that they were burning through billions in cash reserves each month and would be bankrupt in the first half of 2009. Ford and Chrysler are reportedly not far behind.

According to the *Washington Post*: "Economists estimate that a rapid auto industry meltdown could cost up to 3 million jobs—perhaps sending the jobless rate as high as 9.5 percent. It could also result in a bottomless psychology of panic."

This crisis is many years in the making. Over the past decades, the Big Three gave up the majority of the market for small, fuel efficient cars to other manufacturers. Rather than changing with the times and orienting towards more environmentally-friendly technologies or even trying to build more public transportation, they concentrated on more profitable minivans, SUVs and giant pick-up trucks. However, with fuel prices having hit a record high over the summer, the market for these big gas guzzlers has collapsed. Additionally, the financial crisis has made it more difficult for consumers to borrow the money to buy a car.

Since 2006, tens of thousands of jobs in the auto industry have been lost.

Impact on Unions and Workers

Since 2006, tens of thousands of jobs in the auto industry have been lost. According to *The New York Times*: "The downsizing has been harsh. More than 100,000 jobs have disappeared since January at the automakers and their suppliers." In many cases, new hires are only making half as much as the older employees they work next to. There have been massive attacks on retirement benefits, including healthcare benefits for retirees.

Now, in more and more cases, retirement benefits are being paid out not by the company, but by the union through the "Voluntary Employee Beneficiary Association" (VEBA), a union-run trust fund which pays out retirement benefits. It is a real catastrophe that the UAW has taken on this role. Unions exist to represent workers' interests. Running funds like VEBA can put the union leadership in a position of cutting retirees' benefits. Who will stand up for those workers and retirees, when the cuts are coming from the union leadership?

We have to see what is behind the present plan for a bailout. The last bailout in the auto industry was of Chrysler Corporation in 1979. In this deal the UAW leadership agreed to an estimated $203 million in concessions for the workers. This then paved the way for major concessions in wages and benefits for workers in other industries.

In an excellent article by Dan La Botz [Nov. 18, 2008] called "What's to be done about the Auto Industry?" he writes: "The union [UAW] relegated itself to the role of the Big Three's junior partner, then sidekick, and finally hanger on. Fearing to mobilize the members and summon them to struggle, the UAW turned to the Democratic Party to solve its problems. Now we will see what the Democrats do. It will likely be the Chrysler Bailout of 1979 all over again, only writ larger: that is, save what can be saved of the auto companies, let workers go, shred the contract and lower wages."

From the point of view of industry executives and politicians there would be a certain advantage of declaring bankruptcy.

The comments from former Bill Clinton Commerce Secretary Bill Daley, now an Obama economic transition advisor, should be a warning that a Chrysler-like deal might be the most likely outcome. On NBC's "Meet the Press" he said: "They have to do it ... The responsibility is on the auto industry and the unions to come back with a plan."

When you see the word "bailout"—it means: "Either take 'voluntary' concessions or go into bankruptcy." From the point of view of industry executives and politicians there would be a certain advantage of declaring bankruptcy. The companies could legally get out of some of their contractual obligations to workers. The steel industry was the model of this approach, which had a devastating effect on jobs and communities which relied on the steel industry.

Attacks of this type, and attempts to transform the role of unions, are a part of the new business model of the automotive industry. They are trying to make workers pay for the crisis the current corporate ownership and their system has created. They hope to come out of the crisis with a workforce that has little if any benefits and low wages. The situation is already at the point where the wages paid by non-union plants are at a similar level as the new hires at unionized plants.

Devastating Communities

The underlying logic of their system is disastrous for working class people. For the last 40 years the Big Three's corporate ownership have followed one policy—maximize short-term profits. That's what Wall Street demands, that's what investors demand, and that's how the capitalist system operates. The executives of GM, Chrysler and Ford put all their eggs into the basket of the recent short-term sales winner—SUVs. When consumers didn't want to buy them, they added thousands of dollars in incentives. The profits they made were invested in financial companies and partnerships with foreign auto companies. Along with this was a sharp attack on wages and benefits of auto workers. Now they suddenly find themselves in a mess.

In the areas of the Midwest, where the industry is centered, there will be massive job losses, mortgage foreclosures and the destruction of entire communities.

If the industry collapses, it will cost an estimated 250,000 auto jobs, plus an additional 1.5–2.5 million jobs that depend on autoworkers. This will have a devastating effect on an economy that's already facing the highest unemployment rate in 14 years, with some economists predicting unemployment to hit 9–10% [in 2009].

In the areas of the Midwest, where the industry is centered, there will be massive job losses, mortgage foreclosures and the destruction of entire communities. Millions of working families will see their lives devastated.

Union Complicity in the Auto Crisis

The failure of the UAW leadership to present an alternative to the corporate agenda that eventually threatened to destroy the auto industry has been a key problem.

William Serrin, in his book *The Company and the Union* (1973), writes: "Already by the 1950s the UAW leadership was trading off wage and benefit gains for workers in exchange for allowing management to introduce automation and take greater control of workers on the shop floor. The line sped up, but the workers had little recourse. Rebellions by black workers in Detroit and Appalachian workers in Lordstown and Cincinnati in the 1960s could not break the union's partnership with management. General Motors and the UAW had become partners, while the UAW and its members were partners no longer."

The shocking short-sightedness of the UAW leadership also failed to expand the gains won in wages and benefits by auto workers to the wider working class.

William Serrin again describes this issue well: "Today, the UAW does little to attack the many problems workers face in American society: racism, the tax system, sex discrimination, highway safety, factory safety, housing, environmental pollution. It was the sons of the working class that were being claimed by the war in Vietnam, but the UAW did not attack the war until attacking the war was acceptable, even popular ... Since the UAW didn't care about the rest of the working class, the rest of the working class came to resent what it saw as the privileges of UAW members."

While the UAW was moving into a closer and closer "partnership" with management, auto workers saw their living standards and hopes for the future shattered. Hundreds of thousands of layoffs, attacks on health benefits and pensions have been their reward for hot dangerous work in the brutal conditions that still dominate the auto plants in 2008. Only by recreating a fighting union based on control by its membership can auto workers expect to successfully fight back.

The only way to save the good-paying union jobs is to bring the auto industry into public ownership under democratic control and management.

End Corporate Ownership

The auto industry can't be allowed to collapse. At the same time, simply putting tens of billions of taxpayer dollars in the hands of the people who drove the industry into this crisis also doesn't make sense. The auto-industry executives shouldn't be entrusted with any public money.

This crisis shows that the auto industry can't simply continue with business as usual. The only way to save the good-paying union jobs is to bring the auto industry into public ownership under democratic control and management. Decision-making should not be left in the hands of the corporate ownership, or the Democratic or Republican politicians, or government bureaucrats. It should be run by a board consisting of union members, environmentalists, elected representatives of local communities where the plants are located, and the government.

A plan should be drawn up to retool the plants to provide for the transportation, energy and infrastructure needs of the coming decade. A portion of productive capacity should be redirected to plan and produce more environmentally-friendly cars and public transportation, including buses, light rail, high-speed trains and wind turbines, etc. New fuel technology should be integrated into the production system.

To turn around the economy we can't stop at just bringing the auto industry under public ownership. The financial system clearly is not geared towards serving the interests of the vast majority of society but the needs of the millionaires and billionaires. By bringing the big banks under public ownership, funds could be directed to build new environmentally-friendly industries to provide for the long-term needs of society, not a few billionaires. This is the only way to secure a decent future for working people.

14

The Government Should Not Bail Out Deceptive Student Loan Lenders

Stephen Burd

Stephen Burd is a senior research fellow in the Education Policy Program at the New America Foundation, a nonprofit public policy institute. He also serves as the managing editor of Higher Ed Watch, a New America Foundation blog that follows issues relating to higher education.

Some banks have partnered with unregulated vocational schools to offer student loans to mostly at-risk borrowers. Unfortunately, these schools have often folded under questionable circumstances, leaving students to pay off their student loan debts without having finished their curriculum. The banks that made such loans and demand repayment from students who did not get the chance to complete their education should be investigated, and the government should withhold any bailout money from these banks until they are cleared of any wrongdoing in this matter.

Readers of [the Higher Ed Watch blog] will know that we think it would be a major mistake for the U.S. Treasury and Congress to provide bailout funds for private student loan providers—especially, without giving the borrowers of these high-cost loans better consumer protections. To better understand why we think that way, consider the case of Key Bank—which arguably has engaged in some of the most ques-

Stephen Burd, "A 'Key' Reason Not to Bail Out Private Student Loan Providers," NewAmerica.net, December 10, 2008. Reproduced by permission.

tionable private student loan practices of any company. Is it really in the best interest of the government and taxpayers to help companies whose lending practices have put students in such harm's way?

[Key Bank] has denied borrowers basic protections that are in federal law to protect borrowers from being scammed by unscrupulous schools and loan providers.

As we have reported previously [in April 2008], there has been in recent years a proliferation of unlicensed and unaccredited trade schools that do not participate in the federal student aid programs and therefore go largely unregulated. Their growth has been fueled by lenders that have "partnered" with these institutions to provide expensive private loans to the at-risk students these schools tend to attract. The lenders have then turned around and, like subprime mortgage providers, securitized the loans, shifting these high-risk loans onto unsuspecting investors.

One of the most aggressive players in this arena has been Key Bank. Over the last decade, Key Bank has formed exclusive arrangements with dozens of unlicensed trade schools— particularly ones that focus on computer training and flight training. These unregulated schools have required their students to pay for the full cost of their training up front, with tens of thousands of dollars of private loans from Key Bank. Unfortunately, many of these schools, like the Nevada-based Silver State Helicopters (SSH), failed to deliver the education promised and then shut down without warning, leaving their students in the lurch—heavily indebted with expensive private loans and no practical training.

No Protection for Borrowers

In case after case, Key Bank has fought vigorously (and often successfully) to force students to pay back these high-cost loans, despite the fact that the schools closed before the low-income and working class students these institutions tend to attract could receive the training they were promised. In doing so, the corporation has denied borrowers basic protections that are in federal law to protect borrowers from being scammed by unscrupulous schools and loan providers. For example, the bank has routinely omitted from the promissory notes for its private loans a required notice that asserts the borrowers' right to have their loans canceled if a school with which it has "a referring relationship" closes down, is not licensed, or engages in fraud.

Key Bank officials deny any wrongdoing, saying that they cannot be held responsible for mismanagement at the schools with which they work.

Students who attended these unregulated fly-by-night trade schools are fighting back. At least two major lawsuits are moving forward against Key Bank, accusing the company of colluding with disreputable schools to defraud students. They say that Key Bank officials were well aware of problems at these schools but chose to ignore them in order to continue marketing loans to the institutions' students.

Key Bank officials deny any wrongdoing, saying that they cannot be held responsible for mismanagement at the schools with which they work.

Left in the Lurch at Silver State

In May [2008], students in California who attended flight schools run by Silver State Helicopters, a Nevada-based chain that shut down suddenly on Super Bowl Sunday [Feb. 3, 2008], filed a class action lawsuit against Key Bank and several other lenders, seeking to get their private loans discharged.

According to the lawsuit, Key Bank was Silver State's exclusive private student loan provider from 2002 to 2005, a time when the flight school chain grew by "an astounding 2,786 percent." The lawsuit states that the school directed prospective students to apply for private loans from Key Bank to cover the full cost of attendance—nearly $70,000 per student—that they were required to pay upfront before classes started. "The school targeted second career, limited income individuals who, but for the Defendant's loan, lacked the personal financial wherewithal to pay the tuition," the lawsuit states. The willingness of Key Bank to waive its credit requirements to provide these high-cost loans to mostly subprime borrowers served "as a fundamental catalyst for SSH's exponential growth," the document says.

Soon after the students enrolled, however, they realized that the school was ill-equipped to deliver the training that was promised. "SSH was unable to provide the equipment, instructors or maintenance necessary to enable the students to attain their pilot ratings," the lawsuit says. Key Bank was made aware of these problems, the lawsuit states, but continued to help market the school. [In 2005, Key Bank severed its ties to Silver State, forcing the school to find other lending partners to make and service its loans. The flight school chain then forged an exclusive arrangement with Student Loan Xpress and Pennsylvania Higher Education Assistance Agency (PHEAA).]

The lawsuit argues that Key Bank's relationship with Silver State is not an isolated case. Instead it points to similar arrangements the bank has forged with other unaccredited trade schools that also shut down to assert that "Key Bank's involvement with SSH and its treatment of the SSH students is part of a pattern and practice of fraudulent conduct." The lawsuit accuses the bank of violating the federal Racketeer Influenced and [Corrupt] Organizations (RICO) Act by engaging "in a deliberate pattern and practice of aiding and abetting fraudulent vocational schools that aggressively induce students into obtaining loans with Key Bank."

Key Bank officials deny any wrongdoing, saying that they had little involvement with the schools except to provide financing to their students.

TAB Express International Students Fight Back

A second lawsuit—filed by more than 50 former students from TAB Express International, a now-defunct flight school in northern Florida—presents a remarkably similar case to that of the Silver State students.

In June 2005, TAB shut its doors without notice, after Key Bank ended its three-year relationship with the school. Prior to that, the lawsuit states, Key Bank and TAB had "a mutually advantageous relationship" in which the school required students to take out private loans from that lender to attend the institution, according to the lawsuit. "In fact," the lawsuit states, "TAB would not accept cash installments or other loans on behalf of students for their training, and insisted the students instead obtain a loan or loans from Key Bank exclusively."

At the very least, the government should withhold any liquidity aid from Key Bank until it launches a thorough investigation.

Just as at Silver State, students wishing to attend TAB had to take out private loans from Key Bank covering the full cost of attendance—sometimes as much as $100,000—before classes even started. The bank sent the money directly to the school. According to the lawsuit, students were told that their loans would be forgiven after they completed the training and worked for TAB's airline for a period of time.

But soon after enrolling, students became suspicious. "The students became aware of a lack of available instructors, simulators, and aircraft at the flight school as the school continued to increase the number of enrollees," the lawsuit states. Eventually, they realized that "TAB had no airline." The lawsuit says that the students repeatedly brought their concerns to Key Bank officials but were rebuffed, and the lender continued to help market the school to prospective students.

When the deal finally collapsed, the lawsuit says, Key Bank officials tried to convince the students to take advantage of a "train out option" that would have required them to take on more debt and to waive their right to pursue legal action. Most of the students were not persuaded. Now the case is scheduled to go to trial in a state circuit court in March.

Be Careful with Bailout Money

As a result of the credit crunch, Key Bank stopped making private student loans [in] summer [2008]. With Treasury Secretary Henry Paulson intent on bailing out the private loan industry, we fear that the government will rush to the aid of Key Bank, and others like it, without being aware of the provider's questionable past practices.

At the very least, the government should withhold any liquidity aid from Key Bank until it launches a thorough investigation of the serious allegations that have been made by students from dozens of unlicensed schools. We would hope that the bank would be required to discharge the private loans of students from Silver State and TAB International, as well as others who were victims of sham schools with which the lender partnered.

To be clear, we oppose a private loan bailout. But if one is to occur, the government needs to insure that it is not adding fuel to the fire, and encouraging private loan providers to continue harming students and borrowers. It's time to put an end to these types of predatory lending practices, not encourage them.

15

The Government Should Cancel Student Loan Debt

Robert Applebaum

Robert Applebaum is an attorney from New York who formed "Cancel Student Loan Debt to Stimulate the Economy," a group on the Facebook social networking Web site. Applebaum's group contends that middle class workers are overburdened with student loan debt, which keeps these average Americans from helping to revitalize the economy.

The United States must take some action to help citizens reinvigorate the economy. Channeling bailout money to banks and other financial institutions is not the right solution, for it does not encourage these corporations to change their faulty practices. Instead, the government should help Americans directly. One promising way to do this would be to cancel student loan debt. If the government used a portion of the bailout funds to erase this debt, average Americans would have extra spending cash every month that they could pump into the economy.

President [Barack] Obama ... signed into law a $787 billion stimulus package on top of [former President George W.] Bush's grossly mismanaged $700 billion TARP [Troubled Assets Relief Program] bailout from last September [2008]. While many parts of the bill will act to stimulate the economy, many parts of it simply won't.

Tax rebate checks do not stimulate the economy—history shows that people either spend such rebates on paying off

Robert Applebaum, "Cancel Student Loan Debt to Stimulate the Economy," Facebook .com, 2009. Reproduced by permission of the author.

credit card debt, or they simply save them, doing little to nothing to stimulate the economy. Presumably, that is why they were removed from the final version of the bill. The tax cuts that were included, however, amount to a whopping $44 per month for the rest of 2009, decreasing to an even more staggering $33 per month in 2010. This is hardly "relief" as it is likely to help nobody.

The Wall Street financial institutions, auto manufacturers and countless other irresponsible actors have received billions, going on TRILLIONS of taxpayer dollars to bail them out of their self-created mess. This, too, does nothing to stimulate the economy. It merely rewards bad behavior and does nothing to encourage institutional change. There is a better way.

The debt we've accrued to obtain [learning] degrees have crippled our ability to reap the benefits of our educations.

Education Should Be the Key to a Secure Economic Future

How many times have we heard from our leaders in Washington that education is the key to solving all of our underlying societal problems? The so-called "Silver Bullet." For decades, Presidents, Senators and Members of Congress have touted themselves as champions of education, yet they've done nothing to actually encourage the pursuit of one on an individual level.

Some of us have taken advantage of Federal Stafford Loans and other programs, including private loans, to finance higher education, presumably with the understanding that an advanced degree equates with higher earning power in the future. Many of us go into public service after attaining such degrees, something that's also repeatedly proclaimed as something society should encourage. Yet, the debt we've accrued to obtain such degrees have crippled our ability to reap the benefits of our educations, causing many to make the unfortunate choice of leaving public service so as to earn enough money to pay off that debt.

Our economy is in the tank. There isn't an economist alive who doesn't believe that the economy needs stimulating immediately. The only debate now centers on how to go about doing it. While the new stimulus plan contains some worthy provisions, very little of it will have a significant and immediate stimulating effect on the economy. The Obama Administration itself doesn't expect to see an upsurge in the economy until mid-to-late 2010.

Instead of funneling billions, if not trillions of additional dollars to banks, financial institutions, insurance companies and other institutions of greed that are responsible for the current economic crisis, why not allow educated, hardworking, middle-class Americans to get something in return? After all, they're our tax dollars too!

This is not about a free ride. This is about a new approach to economic stimulus, nothing more.

A Plan to Stimulate the Economy Now

Forgiving student loan debt would have an immediate stimulating effect on the economy. Responsible people who did nothing other than pursue a higher education would have hundreds, if not thousands of extra dollars per month to spend, fueling the economy now. Those extra dollars being pumped into the economy would have a multiplying effect, unlike many of the provisions of the new stimulus package. As a result, tax revenues would go up, the credit markets will unfreeze and jobs will be created.

Let me be clear. This is not about a free ride. This is about a new approach to economic stimulus, nothing more. To those who would argue that this proposal would cause the banking system to collapse or make student loans unavailable to future borrowers, please allow me to respond.

I am in no way suggesting that the lending institutions who manage such debts get legislatively shafted by having these assets wiped from their books. The banks and other financial institutions are going to get their money regardless because, in addition to the $700 [billion] TARP bailout, more bailout money is coming their way (stay tuned!)—this proposal merely suggests that educated, hardworking Americans who are saddled with student loan debt should get something in return, rather than sending those institutions another enormous blank check. Because the banks are being handed trillions of dollars anyway, there would be no danger of making funds unavailable to future borrowers.

Many of the vocal nay-sayers who have curiously joined this group seem intent on ignoring the fact that Washington IS going to spend trillions of dollars, likely in the form of handing blank checks over to more and more banks, as a way of getting the economy under control. Normative assessments of how things should be are fine, but they don't reflect reality.

Accepting the premise that Washington will spend trillions of dollars in unprecedented ways (a good portion of which will just be trial and error, since we're in uncharted waters), what is the argument against directly helping middle class people who are struggling, rather than focusing solely on the banks and other financial institutions responsible for the crisis to begin with?

Accepting that there is an aggregate amount of outstanding student loan debt totaling approximately $550–600 billion, (that's billion with a b, not a t), one is forced to ask again, what is the objection to helping real people with real hardships when all we're talking about is a relative drop in the bucket as compared with what will be spent to dig us out of this hole?

All we need is relief from debt that was accrued under the now-false promise that higher education equates with higher earnings.

America Needs to Free Up Money for the Middle Class

In a perfect world, I share these biases towards personal responsibility and having people pay back what they owe, making good on the commitments they've made. But we don't live in a perfect world and the global economy, not just the U.S. economy, is in a downward spiral, the likes of which nobody truly knows how to fix.

This proposal will free up money for hardworking, educated Americans, giving them more money in their pockets every month, addressing the very real psychological aspects of the recession as much as the financial ones. Is it the only answer? No, of course not. But could it help millions of hardworking people who struggle every month to get by? Absolutely. Given the current economic climate, as well as the plans to spend trillions of additional dollars that are in the works, one must wonder what is so objectionable about giving a real helping hand to real people with real struggles.

2009 and the new Obama Administration is supposed to be about change. Nothing in the new economic stimulus package represents a significant departure from the way Washington has always operated—it's merely a different set of priorities on a higher scale, but it's certainly not materially different from any other economic stimulus package passed during the past few decades.

Washington cannot simply print and borrow money to get us out of this crisis. We the People, however, can get this economy moving NOW. All we need is relief from debt that was accrued under the now-false promise that higher education equates with higher earnings.

Free us of our obligations to repay our out-of-control student loan debt and we, the educated, hardworking, middle-class Americans who drive this economy, will spend those extra dollars now.

Organizations to Contact

The editors have compiled the following list of organizations concerned with the issues debated in this book. The descriptions are derived from materials provided by the organizations. All have publications or information available for interested readers. The list was compiled on the date of publication of the present volume; the information provided here may change. Be aware that many organizations take several weeks or longer to respond to inquiries, so allow as much time as possible.

American Enterprise Institute for Public Policy Research (AEI)
1150 Seventeenth St. NW, Washington, DC   20036
(202) 862-5800 • fax: (202) 862-7177
Web site: www.aei.org

AEI is a nonpartisan, public policy institute dedicated to promoting the value of limited government, private industry, personal responsibility, and government accountability. The organization generally espouses a belief in the ability of free markets to overcome economic downturn and instability; however, in the wake of the recent financial crisis, AEI scholars have admitted the value of nationalizing certain economic cornerstones, such as American banks, in an effort to stabilize the economy. Articles examining the pros and cons of federal involvement in private industry can be read in AEI's monthly publication *The American*, with additional articles, commentary, and testimony available on the AEI Web site.

Cato Institute
1000 Massachusetts Ave. NW, Washington, DC   20001-5403
(202) 842-0200 • fax: (202) 842-3490
Web site: www.cato.org

A libertarian public policy think tank, the Cato Institute advocates limited government involvement in both the economic and social lives of American citizens and companies. With regards to the government's decision to bail out private industry in light of the ongoing financial crisis, Cato cautions against extensive government involvement, warning that when the government intervenes in the matters of private industry, the potential exists for unconstitutional imposition of restrictions on individuals and corporations. Official Cato publications include the quarterly magazine, *Regulation*, and the bimonthly newsletter, *Cato Policy Report*. Articles from these as well as transcripts and online commentary can be accessed at Cato's Web site.

Center for American Progress (CAP)
1333 H St. NW, 10th Fl., Washington, DC   20005
(202) 682-1611 • fax: (202) 682-1867
e-mail: progress@americanprogress.org
Web site: www.americanprogress.org

CAP was founded in 2003 to advance a progressive alternative to the conservative rhetoric and ideas present in American politics. The center promotes public policy that restores America's position as a global leader, focuses on the creation and use of clean energy technology, provides economic opportunity for all, and offers universal health care to all Americans. CAP believes the bailout of private industry to be a necessary step in reestablishing the stability of the American economy and promoting future growth. Analysis of recent and current bailout legislation can be read on the organization's Web site.

Economic Policy Institute (EPI)
1333 H St. NW, Suite 300, East Tower
Washington, DC   20005-4707
(202) 775-8810 • fax: (202) 775-0819
e-mail: epi@epi.org
Web site: www.epi.org

EPI, a nonprofit think tank, seeks to ensure that the interests of low and middle-income workers are represented and considered in the national debate about economic policy. The institute views the government bailout of private industry as essential to ensuring the stability of the American economy and the continued employment of many low- and middle-income workers who would be among the first to lose their jobs should certain industries declare bankruptcy. Additionally, EPI favors a financial industry bailout plan with conditions that protect the taxpayers, whose money will be used to fund the plan, from significant losses. EPI publications and reports can be read online.

Federal Reserve
20th St. and Constitution Ave. NW, Washington, DC   20551
Web site: www.federalreserve.gov

Established on December 23, 1913, the Federal Reserve, or the Fed, is the central bank of the United States. The Fed influences money and credit conditions, oversees banking institutions and regulates their activity, aids in the maintenance of economic stability by containing risk, and provides financial services to the U.S. government and public. Members of the board have provided testimony and speeches concerning the current financial crisis and bailout measures, transcripts of which are available online.

Foundation for Economic Education (FEE)
30 S Broadway, Irvington-on-Hudson, NY   10533
(800) 960-4FEE • fax: (914) 591-8910
Web site: www.fee.org

FEE is an organization, founded in 1946, to promote the principles of free market economics and the "freedom philosophy." FEE has criticized the different bailout packages that have provided government aid to struggling private companies throughout the current recession, maintaining that free market economics, not government intervention, will provide the stimulus the economy needs to rebound and stabilize. These articles and others assessing the financial crisis can be read on the FEE Web site.

Heritage Foundation

214 Massachusetts Ave. NE, Washington, DC   20002-4999
(202) 546-4400 • fax: (202) 546-8328
e-mail: info@heritage.org
Web site: www.heritage.org

The Heritage Foundation is a conservative public policy research institute that seeks to advance national government policies developed using the ideas of free market economics, limited government involvement in private industry, individual freedom, and a strong national defense. The organization opposes the use of federal money to bail out private industry, maintaining that government spending neither stimulates economic growth nor encourages fledgling private companies to improve their business models. Current Heritage reports and commentary can be read on the foundation's Web site.

National Bureau of Economic Research (NBER)

1050 Massachusetts Ave., Cambridge, MA   02138-5398
(617) 868-3900 • fax: (617) 868-2742
Web site: www.nber.org

Since its founding in 1920, NBER has been working to provide unbiased, accurate information about the state of the national and global economy to policymakers, professionals, and academics. In the current situation of global economic crisis, NBER has worked to publish and disseminate reports providing explanations of how the situation occurred and what options exist to solve current problems. Publications of the organization include the monthly *NBER Digest* and the quarterly *NBER Reporter*. Copies of these publications as well as other articles and reports can be accessed online.

Reason Foundation

3415 S Sepulveda Blvd., Suite 400, Los Angeles, CA   90034
(310) 391-2245 • fax: (310) 391-4395
Web site: http://reason.org

Reason Foundation was founded in 1968 to encourage the development and implementation of policies based on the Libertarian principles of free market economics, individual liberty, and the rule of law. As such, Reason has generally opposed the recent bailouts of private industry, arguing that competition and innovation coupled with a free market economy are the best solution to the current economic crisis, not increased government spending that rewards failing industries. Comprehensive coverage of the ongoing recession and proposed bailout and stimulus bills can be found on the foundation's Web site. *Reason Magazine* is the monthly publication of the organization.

United States Government Accountability Office (GAO)
414 G St. NW, Washington, DC   20548
(202) 512-3000
e-mail: contact@gao.gov
Web site: www.gao.gov

As the investigative arm of the U.S. government, the GAO serves as a watchdog, ensuring that government policies benefit the American people. Currently, the GAO has published numerous reports outlining the causes of the current recession and analyzing policies being developed and implemented to combat the ongoing crisis. Copies of these reports can be accessed at the GAO Web site.

Bibliography

Books

Bill Bamber   *Bear-Trap: The Fall of Bear Stearns and the Panic of 2008.* New York: Brick Tower, 2008.

Richard Bitner   *Confessions of a Subprime Lender: An Insider's Tale of Greed, Fraud, and Ignorance.* New York: Wiley, 2008.

Niall Ferguson   *The Ascent of Money: A Financial History of the World.* New York: Penguin, 2008.

Charles P. Kindleberger, Robert Aliber, and Robert Solow   *Manias, Panics, and Crashes: A History of Financial Crises.* New York: Wiley, 2005.

Paul Krugman   *The Return of Depression Economics and the Crisis of 2008.* New York: Norton, 2008.

Michael Lewis   *Panic: The Story of Modern Financial Insanity.* New York: Norton, 2008.

Adam Michaelson   *The Foreclosure of America: The Inside Story of the Rise and Fall of Countrywide Home Loans, the Mortgage Crisis, and the Default of the American Dream.* New York: Berkeley, 2009.

Charles R. Morris   *The Two Trillion Dollar Meltdown: Easy Money, High Rollers, and the Great Credit Crash.* Jackson, TN: PublicAffairs, 2009.

Paul Muolo and Mathew Padilla   *Chain of Blame: How Wall Street Caused the Mortgage and Credit Crisis.* New York: Wiley, 2008.

Kevin Phillips   *Bad Money: Reckless Finance, Failed Politics, and the Global Crisis of American Capitalism.* New York: Viking, 2008.

Barry Ritholtz, Bill Fleckenstein, and Aaron Task   *Bailout Nation: How Greed and Easy Money Corrupted Wall Street and Shook the World Economy.* New York: Wiley, 2009.

Robert J. Shiller   *The Subprime Solution: How Today's Global Financial Crisis Happened, and What to Do about It.* Princeton, NJ: Princeton University Press, 2008.

Gary H. Stern and Ron J. Feldman   *Too Big to Fail: The Hazards of Bank Bailouts.* Washington, DC: Brookings Institution Press, 2004.

Thomas E. Woods Jr. and Ron Paul   *Meltdown: A Free-Market Look at Why the Stock Market Collapsed, the Economy Tanked, and Government Bailouts Will Make Things Worse.* Washington, DC: Regnery, 2009.

U.S. Government   *BailOut 2008: The Full Details on the Historic Wall Street Government Rescue Plan.* Charleston, SC: BiblioBazaar, 2008.

Periodicals

Stanley Bing — "Stimulate Me!" *Fortune*, March 2, 2009.

Christopher Cox — "We Need a Bailout Exit Strategy," *Wall Street Journal*, December 11, 2008.

Peter Coy, Dean Foust, and Theo Francis — "Nationalization: Who Would Bear the Pain?" *BusinessWeek*, March 9, 2009.

E.J. Dionne Jr. — "Keeping Up Appearances," *Commonweal*, February 27, 2009.

David Dreman — "Bailout Blues," *Forbes*, November 17, 2008.

Thomas L. Friedman — "Start Up The Risk-Takers," *New York Times*, February 22, 2009.

Stephen Gandel — "America's Broken Banks," *Time*, February 9, 2009.

Jeffrey E. Garten — "The Big Bang of Bailouts," *Newsweek*, December 22, 2008.

John D. Geanakopolos and Susan P. Koniak — "Matters of Principle," *New York Times*, March 5, 2009.

Ron Gettelfinger — "We Must Save the Auto Industry," *U.S. News & World Report*, December 15, 2008.

William Greider — "The Crisis Is Global," *Nation*, February 2, 2009.

Jeb Hensarling   "Detroit Bailout Hurts Everyone Else," *Human Events*, January 5, 2009.

Tamara E. Holmes   "Wall Street Bailout?" *Black Enterprise*, December 2008.

William F. Jasper   "Bailout Mania!" *New American*, January 5, 2009.

Patrick Krey   "The Bailout and the Constitution," *New American*, November 24, 2008.

Paul Krugman   "Obama's Bailout," *Rolling Stone*, March 3, 2009.

Arthur B. Laffer   "The Age of Prosperity Is Over," *Wall Street Journal*, October 27, 2008.

Mark Levinson   "The Economic Collapse," *Dissent*, Winter 2009.

Michael E. Lewitt   "Make It Work," *New Republic*, November 5, 2008.

Heidi N. Moore   "The Benefits of GM Bankruptcy," *Wall Street Journal*, February 23, 2009.

Adam Nagourney   "Bracing for a Bailout Backlash," *New York Times*, March 16, 2009.

Alan Reynolds   "Worse Than a Bailout—A Blunder," *National Review*, October 20, 2008.

Emma Rothschild   "Can We Transform the Auto-Industrial Society?" *New York Review of Books*, February 26, 2009.

Randy Salzman   "Does the Bailout Spree Signal the
                     End of Democracy?" *Christian
                     Science Monitor*, December 22, 2008.

Judith F.   "Are Executives Paid Too Much?"
Samuelson and   *Wall Street Journal*, February 26,
Lynn A. Stout   2009.

Robert J.   "The Bailout Isn't a Morality Play,"
Samuelson   *Newsweek*, February 16, 2009.

Ron Scherer   "Are Jobless Next to Need a Bailout?"
                     Christian Science Monitor, November
                     10, 2008.

Joseph E. Stiglitz   "A Bailout That Works," *Nation*,
                     March 23, 2009.

David Von Drehle   "House of Cards," *Time*, March 9,
and Maya Curry   2009.

Fareed Zakaria   "There's More to Fear Than Fear,"
                     Newsweek, February 2, 2009.

Mortimer B.   "We Deserve a Better Bailout," *U.S.
Zuckerman   News & World Report*, October 13,
                     2008.

Index